'Updatism' and the Understanding of Time and History

'Updatism' and the Understanding of Time and History

A Theory for the Twenty-First Century

Edited by

Mateus Henrique de Faria Pereira and Valdei Lopes de Araujo

BLOOMSBURY ACADEMIC
LONDON • NEW YORK • OXFORD • NEW DELHI • SYDNEY

BLOOMSBURY ACADEMIC
Bloomsbury Publishing Plc
50 Bedford Square, London, WC1B 3DP, UK
1385 Broadway, New York, NY 10018, USA
29 Earlsfort Terrace, Dublin 2, Ireland

BLOOMSBURY, BLOOMSBURY ACADEMIC and the Diana logo are trademarks of
Bloomsbury Publishing Plc

First published in Great Britain 2024

Cover image: Social Media Life (© Michael Walker / Getty Images)

A catalogue record for this book is available from the British Library.

A catalog record for this book is available from the Library of Congress.

ISBN: HB: 978-1-3504-1071-8
PB: 978-1-3504-1072-5
ePDF: 978-1-3504-1073-2
eBook: 978-1-3504-1074-9

Typeset by Deanta Global Publishing Services, Chennai, India

To find out more about our authors and books visit www.bloomsbury.com and sign up for
our newsletters.

Contents

Illustrations

Acknowledgements

Expressing gratitude to the multiple interlocutors is an excellent way to introduce a book that emerged from numerous discussions and conversations, while also acknowledging the colleagues who have aided us in overcoming the adversities of the unfortunate political situation prevailing in Brazil from 2018 to 2022. Their invaluable assistance has facilitated the development and refinement of this book.

The concept of updating as a starting point for exploring the nature of time emerged from a lengthy WhatsApp conversation between the authors in October 2015, while one of them was travelling by bus from Porto Alegre to Pelotas. The argument gained momentum through the message updates, which were both tools and catalysts for stimulating and supporting their thinking. Interestingly, a significant portion of the discussion unfolded while one or both of the authors were on the move. Perhaps the suspension of daily life allowed them to contemplate this experience more deeply. It is worth noting that not every form of updating is updatist, and as this book delves into the potential dangers of updatism, it is essential to clarify this distinction from the outset.

Parts of this text were presented at various academic events, including a mini-workshop in Ghent, Belgium, hosted by the research group coordinated by Berber Bervenage, and the II International Network Meeting for Theory of History (INTH) held in Ouro Preto, Brazil, in August 2016. On both occasions, the argument was enriched by fruitful debates with fellow scholars. An initial comprehensive version of the paper was also presented at the Institute Casa de Leitura Dirce Cortes Riedel, in the State University of Rio de Janeiro (UERJ), in 2017. We express our gratitude to those who attended these events, especially to João Cezar de Castro Rocha for the invitation and his generous contributions. The section on Lyotard was inspired by one of his comments. We also had the opportunity to discuss some of the book's ideas at the invitation of Mara Rodrigues at UFRGS and during the 3rd Meeting of the group 'History (In)disciplined' in the first half of 2018, where we received valuable critical feedback.

We would also like to thank our colleagues at the Studies in History of Historiography and Modernity (NEHM), the Brazilian Society of Theory and History of Historiography (SBTHH), as well as our colleagues from the Department of History of the Universidade Federal de Ouro Preto (UFOP); our undergraduate and graduate students; in particular, our friends: Alexandre Avelar, Ana Mónica Lopes, André Freixo, André Voigt, Anita Lucchesi, André Ramos, Beatriz Vieira, Carol Monay, Caroline Bauer, Daniel Joni, Dalton Sanches, Daniel Faria, Daniel Pinha, Fabio Wasserman, Eduardo Ferraz Felippe, Fernando Nicolazzi, Francisco Gouvea, Helena Mollo, André Ramos, Guilherme Bianchi, Luna Halabi, Mariana Fontes, Mario Marcello Neto, Guilherme Norton, Henrique Estrada, Henrique Gaio, Luana Melo, Géssica Guimarães Gaio, Julio Bentivoglio, Thiago Brito, Luisa Rauter, Luiz Estevam (Duda), Maria da Glória Oliveira, Mateus Reis, Marcelo Abreu, Marcelo Rangel, Pedro dos Santos, Pedro Teles Silveira, Rebeca Gontijo, Rodrigo Turin, Sérgio da Mata, Thamara Rodrigues, Temístocles Cezar, Thiago Nicodemo, Verônica M. Pereira, Yuri Araújo and, in particular, Walderez Ramalho for the careful reading of one of the last versions of the manuscript. We also thank our colleagues and students involved in the editorial work of Revista História da Historiografia: Fábio Franzini, Arthur Avila, Alejandro Eujanian, Augusto Ramires, Marianna Melo and Rodrigo Machado.

For the English language edition, we thank the two reviewers who read and commented with great precision and generosity on the initial text. Many of their suggestions were incorporated into the book in its current version. One of the features of this research was its grounding in the reading, debating and production of texts in more than one national language. Whether in the concept of updating, or in the intricate reading of Western philosophical categories, a substantial part of the argument would not have been possible without the oscillation of the same idea or experience in different linguistic expressions. Therefore, it was essential to maintain the use not only of reading the same text in various languages and even different translations into the same language but also of composing the argument being shaped by this consonance/dissonance of meanings and words.

We also thank the Brazilian agencies that finance this research, CAPES, CNPq, FAPEMIG and UFOP.

Preface

Essay on the (un)updated potentials of thought and time

'Il est temps que vous le sachiez: je suis moi aussi un contemporain.'
(Ossip Mandelstam, Minuit dans Moscou)[1]

From: Valdei Araujo <valdei354@gmail.com>
Date: Wednesday, September 26, 2018 09:57
To: Temístocles Cezar <t.cezar@ufrgs.br>, Mateus Pereira <matteuspereira@gmail.com>

Subject: Book Updatism
Dear, good morning!
Attached, it follows, finally, a final version of the book on Updatism. We want to release it through SBTHH's seal (. . .).
But the reason for this e-mail is to invite you to write the preface, because the little book owes much to your encouragement and dialogue. We would be very happy if you could collaborate.
A big hug,

Valdei & Mateus.
From: Temístocles Cezar <t.cezar@ufrgs.br>
Date: Wednesday, October 10, 2018 05:28
To: Valdei Araujo <valdei354@gmail.com>, Mateus Pereira <matteuspereira@gmail.com>

Subject: Re: Book Updatism
Dear friends,
Good morning!
Your invitation, aside from being an honor that provides me much satisfaction, is a challenge in and about time. Between the University's

activities, the daily family life and a quick trip to Buenos Aires, and, above all, involved, like most of us, in the dilemmas of our current time, I thought, at first, about trying to cast, by way of preface, a look on the 'current world', as did Paul Valéry in *Regards sur le monde actuel*, whose first edition dates from 1931.[2] Much pretension and so little time. . . More than writing the preface I would like to talk, to exchange ideas, to hear you, to write like an old friend and not just a colleague who isn't adept to social media, but who attends with certain regularity the virtual world, not as much to *update* myself ('not all forms of updating are updatist', you prevent!), but as a necessary work tool and as a heuristic device to try to understand what goes by my eyes, what disturbs so many people that are close to me, what seems to have no rest, tiredness or limit, what leaves so many people 'under the skin', 'what would it be'?

Because of an old formation habit, it is not our muse, nor the *Oração ao tempo* (remember? Por seres tão inventivo/ E pareceres contínuo/ Tempo, tempo, tempo, tempo/ És um dos deuses mais lindos. . .) but another orator, Augustine, comes to my mind when I have to think about time. However, in this moment, I remembered a more recent confession, written by Robert A. Rosenstone: 'Shouldn't we historians know from the history of History that all our stories – the ones we live and the ones we write – will eventually be outmoded, updated, and rewritten, and different versions take their place?'[3] *Updatism* shows how this updatist gear is not a mere epiphenomenon of the historical method, surpassing the confessional requirement of historiography on renewing itself, when launching a rigorous approach of the concept, concomitantly continuous and discontinuous, simultaneous and non-simultaneous, and not alien to everyday experience.

You aim to 'demonstrate that updatism is the temporal dimension that emerges in those societies imprisoned by the structures of infinite expansion.' Rather than considering that the now of the present (*atual*) implies only one deference ('i.e. deference to the past as a priority, as an authority') or in a postponement ('i.e. the constant postponement of historical recognition through its predisposition to keep updating and re-evaluating knowledge already known')[4] of the processes of historicization, the analysis of *updatism* in the proposed terms leads us, through a dialogue with Lyotard, Gumbrecht, Hartog, Heidegger, Chateaubriand, among others, to rethink the limits of this late historicism.[5]

Even considering that the 'pressure to be up to date, to be contemporaneous with a naturalized time as an external force, is not foreign to historicist modernity' (Mandelstam!), and that the updatist drive may even reinforce the historicist dream of the virtual plunge into an inexorable idea of inescapable universal history (the possibility of the unlimited connection with everything and everyone), in which the tyrannies of the present, the ruin of anonymity or the elongated melancholy of the moderns would be symptoms, you do not fail to notice gaps (anti-historicists?), being, at least for me, the most important: 1. the ability to disentangle the current (*atual*) from the present that the concept implies when it 'claims forces of the past (and the future?) as more updated than the present'; 2. and the 'flexibilization of identities' that allow a kind of citizenship of translations from which a greater openness to the multiplication of genders transcends the old and confining categories of the masculine, the feminine, the human, and the nonhuman.

Updatism puts into perspective not only the historicist contingencies, but the dissatisfaction of generational inadequacy with the current ways of managing the world of life. Thus, to the lamentation of Gumbrecht, which does not conceal, in my point of view, a pertinent criticism to the present moment, to the presentism without frontiers of Hartog, which remains a prudent and valid appreciation of a way of temporizing time, which does not make them immune to contestation, as you point out with great elegance and acuity, I would like to propose alternative questions that are related to the non-native digital generation. While for Gumbrecht the landing of the airplane in the airports of the world and the gesture of the passengers immediately getting their phones and connecting as quickly as possible is an indicator of a worrying (and why not distressing) dependence on virtual presence, the cover of Hartog's book on *Presentism* is a photo of Barcelona airport which, he confided to me, means the displacement in the present of the similar to the same (*du pareil au même*). From this angle, as you say, yes, '*updatism would be a hypertrophy of meaning*.'

In addition, a realization that *updatism* 'is experienced as a quasi-magical belief in the reproduction of reality' brings to the debate a pretentious vigorous theme. If, in the field of historiography, photography and cinema have already been or have been seen as reliable representations of the real, in the updatist dimension and its digital attendants, in which photos and films are subsumed, the modalities of belief in the same extent as they widen, since photos and films are supposedly digitally stored forever, they are, despite the constant demands of updating the system, in the imminence of irrecoverable loss of data and unwanted invasions of privacy. Will file and memory still be fundamental to the belief on real-time representation? Would it not be prudent and desirable to develop an aesthetic of loss?

It is also related to the generational division (which multiplies itself in other strata of social time) the problem that you define as the 'right to obsolescence', something close to what I call the right to anonymity. To these rights, I would add the right to error. Let me tell a little story. I was dining at a couple of elderly friends' house who have been married for over 50 years. He, as she characterizes him, is modern: he has a trendy cell phone, Facebook, Instagram, Twitter. We were talking about an old French movie, whose main actor's name I could not remember. Among them there was no consensus. For her it was one, for him another. After a heated argument, in which I was only a witness, he took out his iPhone, consulted Google and showed her and me the photo and the name of the actor on the screen of the cell phone, he said: it was a third name! Continuous act, she declared: nobody has the right to error anymore! Discounting her ordinary impatience with her husband, however much of my studies of ancient cynicism and modern skepticism have accustomed me to doubt, I was unprepared to meditate immediately on the impact of uncertainty and certainty on the order of practical life. I spent a lot of time thinking about the scene without finding exactly the terms to describe my disquietude with a phrase which I thought, initially, was almost unpleasant and apparently unimportant. Through *Updatism* I have been able to insert 'the right to error' in a broader context of inquiries, including thinking of error as an (un)updated variant of the present.

Dear friends, I read part of the book in the *Centro Cultural de la Memoria Haroldo Conti*, one of the buildings that make up the *Espacio memoria y derechos humanos*, ex-Esma, in Buenos Aires, one of the clandestine centers of detention, torture and extermination during the Argentine military dictatorship, while awaiting ML who participated in a seminar.[6] There is no denying that this visitation added to the expectation of the election in Brazil, only three days later, influenced my reading too much. The blue sky and the sun that timidly heated the green grass contrasted, paradoxically, with the oppressive climate that did not relieve the presence of the past. I read the chapter about *Black Mirror* (about a near future or about updatist movements), whose sketch I already knew, and that in an event where one of you presented it, I had related to the problem of sleep and the wake of Descartes. In this second moment, when reading that 'updatism produces the sensation that everything that matters is or will be available and present,' I almost unadvisedly associated it with that creature you define as 'an almost-person, or a person abstracted from their human condition,' to bodies mutilated by intolerance that made human beings metonymy of themselves, temporary beings of a cruel metaphysics of existence.

This time and space that has been updated in me, of course brought with it sadness, bitterness and apprehension as to our return and the Sunday of elections. However, I had read a few months ago a book about the relations between the present time, art and politics, of three authors that I did not know and were presented to me by Hartog, who, in explaining their project, wrote something that made me think of a third dimension of updatism: '(. . .) Nos temps obscurs sont surtout des temps qui se préparent. Il naît de là une impatience, afin que tout ce qui est déjà là, potentiellement, s'actualise. C'est à cette actualisation que travaille la pensée potentielle.'[7]

If, as you say, '*the updatist world is not only the best possible world, it is the only possible world, its constant updating does not open space for the new as discontinuity. The new is a catastrophic failure in the system,*' so the potentiality of your thinking has created, like a computer virus, a new or alternative slit in this temporal structure. For this Trojan-Horse-of-Free-Thinking, there is still no antivirus capable of stopping it! But when you feel it around do not hesitate to press the key: #ELENão!

Thank you so much for the opportunity to read you first handed, for the patience and for your friendship.

Strong hug,

From Temistocles

Notes

1 MANDELSTAM, Ossip. Œuvres poétiques I. Paris: Le Bruit du temps/La Dogana, 2018, p. 405.

2 VALÉRY, Paul. Regards sur le monde actuel et autres essais. Paris: Gallimard, 1998.

3 ROSENSTONE, Robert A. Confessions of a Postmodern (?) Historian. In: MUNSLOW, Alan (edited by). Authoring the past: writing and rethinking history. London and New York: Routledge, 2013, p. 141.

4 DAVIES, Martin L. Imprisoned by History. Aspects of Historicized Life. London and New York: Routledge, 2010, p. 214.

5 For an analysis, safeguarding the contextual differences, but resembling the critical perspective of historicism, see: CHAKRABARTY, Dipesh. Provincializing Europe: postcolonial thought and historical difference. Princeton: Princeton University Press, 2000.

6 XI Seminario Internacional Políticas de la Memoria: Memoria subalternas, memorias rebeldes. Esma: Escuela de Mecanica de la Armada.

7 TOLEDO, Camille de; IMHOFF, Aliocha; QUIRÓS, Kantuta. Les potentiels du temps. Art & politique. Paris: Manuella Éditions, 2016, p. 15.

Introduction

The emergence of the word 'update'

In 2016, the jornalist E. Cantanhêde wrote in a Brazilian newspaper: "As effective president, Temer will update the country". The use of the word 'update' in the journalist's phrase can express a subtle and subterranean shift of experience: a relevant displacement in the modern forms of meaning historical time. What temporal changes allowed the replacement (such as overlap, substitution, synonymy) of the word modernization for updating? Taking into account the well-known criticism to the conceptualization of categories such as 'presentism' (François Hartog) or the 'broad present' (Gumbrecht), we seek to think about this displacement in the experience of time through the category *updatism*, a neologism in the English language. This book is an attempt to put together a series of fragments of reflection around this category, so that, in the end, we can better understand our time and the historical forms of the updatings that have not yet been studied.

English-language etymological dictionaries date the current use of the word 'update' between 1940 and 1945. A search on Ngram, a Google tool that offers the frequency of words or phrases in the huge database of books scanned by the company, reveals a few isolated occurrences throughout the nineteenth century of the word 'update'. At the beginning of the twentieth century, we find cases of the use of the expression with the sense of 'updating', to bring a list or a knowledge to a more complete state. But it is effectively between 1960 and 1970 that the occurrences multiply and the use associated with computer culture begins to better define its semantic field. In a 1967 prospectus from the Defense Technical Information Center, a software named *update* promised to be 'a temporary solution to the basic problem that the entire data system faces in a real-time environment: total loss of all the unprocessed data during error-induced diagnostic recovery modes' (Cameron 1967). In other words, any data imputed to the system became simultaneously 'current', recorded and stored at the same time as it was executed. Thus, as early as 1967 we may have a quick idea of one of the updatist utopias, a time when there would be no distance between action and its integration into an ever-updated system, always in the present state, meaning that the actions that would be passed would remain available without the necessity to decide on their relevance. Therefore, when everything can be saved and retrieved in real time, the classic mechanisms of memory and forgetting can become obsolete or automated.

The word 'atualismo' (updatism) entered Portuguese dictionaries in the mid-twentieth century, but in a specialized sense, as a term of geology or to designate the philosophy of mind of Giovanni Gentile (1987), developed in the early twentieth century and initially designated as 'actual idealism'. This book will use the word 'updatism' as an analytical category that summarizes the historical phenomena we investigate by focusing our research on the history of 'update' and 'updating' forms of temporalization. For the purpose of our research, we noticed that the word 'updating' extends its semantic field, especially since the 1960s. The dictionaries announced in their new editions that they were revised and enlarged and, in regard to this term, they abandoned the idea of growth to announce their *updating*. In the Dictionary of the Portuguese Language Caldas Aulete, since the 1950s the verb 'atualizar (to up date) already had some relation of synonymy with 'to modernize'. From the 1960s and 1970s the adjective *updated* entered into the dictionaries and it means to be aware, connected, with what happens in the present moment.

In contemporary English dictionaries we find a field of synonyms for the form of the verb 'to update' that is closer to the phenomena we intend to highlight throughout this book. In general, the verb is synonymous with renewing, modernizing, restoring, rejuvenating and revising. Although less diffused and with another sense, there is in English the word 'actualism', derived from 'actual', real in the sense of effective, which did not absorb the phenomena that we would like to emphasize with the expression 'updatism'.

In Figure 1, we compare the evolution of the update lexicon in the English language base of Google Ngram[1] and we can verify that the frequency of the word accelerates in the mid-1960s, apparently receiving part of the semantic value of older concepts already used to characterize improvement or positive dynamics in a certain state, such as 'progress' and 'improvement'. The upward curve of 'update' seems to follow the new reality of the computer universe,[2] as we can see in the increment of words like 'web', 'virtual' and 'digital'.

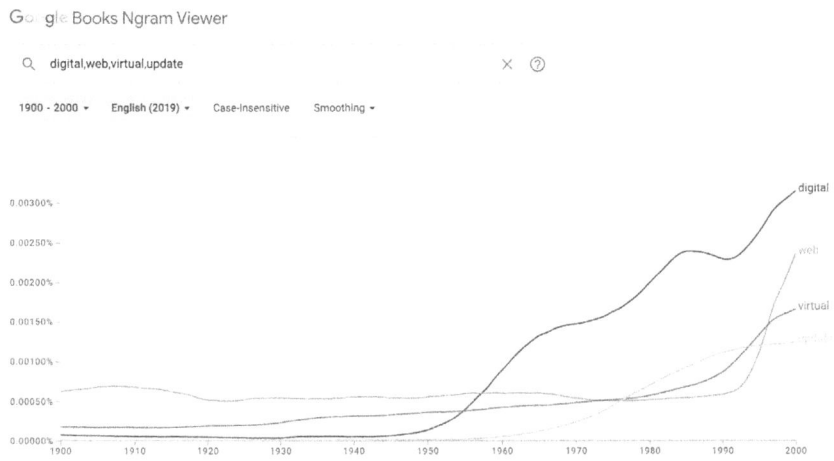

Figure 1 Frequency of digital, web, virtual and update words in the English-language base of Google Ngram. *Source*: Google Ngram, accessed on 19 July 2018.

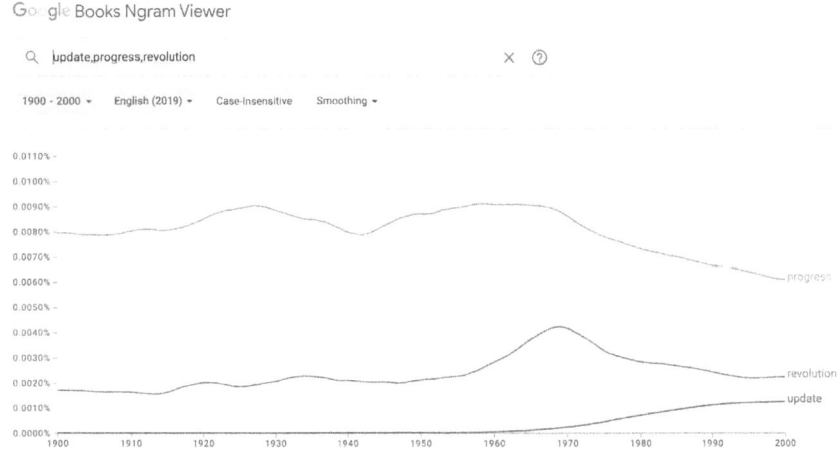

Figure 2 Frequency of progress, evolution and update words in the English-language base of Google Ngram. *Source*: Google Ngram, accessed on 19 July 2018.

We also see in Figure 2 that the frequency of updating increases, while that of some classical modern concepts like 'progress' and 'revolution' decreases.

The term 'updatism', which we propose as a category to define certain features of contemporary temporality, is found in few internet sites and it is most often used in forums about games, fanfictions, vlogs or blogs as a kind of brand for posts with the main function of updating a topic. It appears as a spontaneous and marginal variation of 'update', translating the difficulty of making current the 'real time' of the experience in these digital environments, since the desire or the need of being updated threatens to imprison the user in the stream of the latest news. In the limit, there would be no difference between the time lived and its updating and display.[3]

In the fifth edition of the *American Heritage Dictionary*, the entry 'update' is defined in the verb and noun functions. As a verb, the word can indicate the act of changing something, so as to bring it into the 'present day', the current one: to update a book, to update the files and to inform someone with the latest news. The expression 'latest information' used in the subscription process is the superlative form, which may also appear as a noun, as in the phrase 'the latest in electronic gadgetry', also brought into the exemplification.[4] The current as the last, the most recent and, because of that, the best.

Wednesday, April 14, 2010
UPDATISM
Wow
Woah
Helloooooooo
Its been a little while since we last conversed, a thousand apologies things have been a bit mad of late, i'll explain:

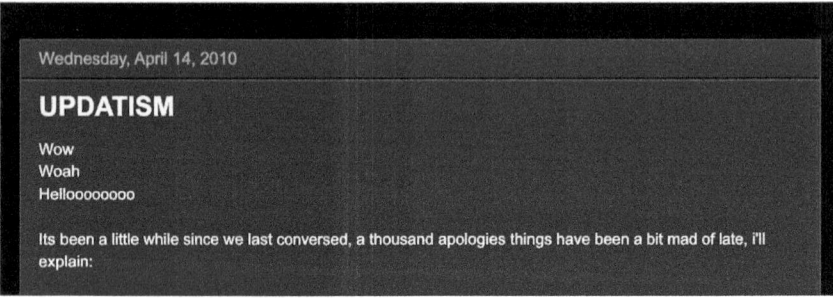

Figure 3 Blogspot site using the word 'updatism' as a title. *Source*: Updatism.blogspot .com, accessed on 25 September 2018.

Tweet
Patrick McFadin
@PatrickMcFadin
Updatism: The optimistic feeling you get when installing an OS update "Maybe this will fix the random problem I've been having with my computer"
Disappontdate: When it doesn't
Traduzir Tweet
3:23 PM · 11 de jun de 2018

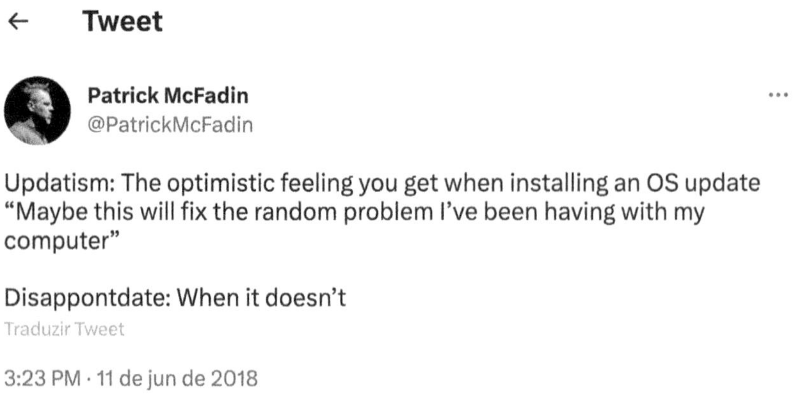

Figure 4 Tweet from Patrick McFadin using the neologism Updatism. *Source*: https://twitter.com/PatrickMcFadin/status/1006240518336987137, accessed on 25 September 2018.

Updating is opposed not only to uncurrent, but to the outdated as obsolete. According to Serge Latouche (2015), programmed obsolescence is at the centre of contemporary societies addicted to growth. In what follows, we will try to demonstrate that updatism is the temporal dimension that emerges in those societies imprisoned by the structures of infinite expansion.

Is there any relation between the growing centrality of the word 'update' and the diffusion of *gadgets*? Apparently yes. As is known, in the 1970s, Lacan began to think about gadgets. For him, they are objects of consumption as if they were 'desires' of the capitalist logic produced by the techno-scientific knowledge. One consequence is the production of commodity-subjects. For Hassan (1998), as 'products of technoscience', these objects have their existence linked to the flow of consumption; they would have automatism as one of their identitarian traits, not only dispensing human control, but also rendering the latter obsolete and even undesirable.

The gadget seems to be a special updatist object, marked by quick obsolescence and, for that reason, it has more value not only for being physically new, but rather because it carries higher updating value. Today we can buy a cell phone or any other *new* object without being *current*, the access to what is current/updated is decided by hierarchies of class, the geopolitics of race, gender, etc. Surrendering to the automatism of the gadget, accepting its automatic updates sold no longer as a product, but as a service, seems to be an inescapable condition of the potentiality-of-being current/updated.

Update may also name a report or narrative that aims to update information about a particular event or process, or to make something more modern, to modernize, always with the sense of improving it or making it correspond to the most recent time, to that which is fashionable. In any case, the pressure to be up to date, to be contemporary with a naturalized time as an external force, is not foreign to historicist modernity. The phenomenon of the pressure of fashion was already socially described in the nineteenth century, for example, in Baudelaire, as a force from which one could not escape without consequences (Agamben 2009, p. 66). For the aforementioned Serge Latouche, obsolescence programmed as a generalized form would be an American invention of the first decades of the twentieth century (2015, pp. 51–5).

However, since the nineteenth century this pressure for being current was tempered by collectively shared images that seemed to make sense and stabilize the changing; institutions and new *professionals* emerged to guide the citizen in his/her task of being inside a time that seemed external, whether it was the time of the nation, the modern or civilized time (Zermeño-Padilla 2008).

As these mediating orientations weakened, the pressure to be in time accelerates to the point of becoming paradoxical. The meeting with oneself or with his/her time, which had seemingly stable places and a training circuit, now seems to be always postponed or obsolete. A positive aspect is the flexibilization of identities, which helps us to think of phenomena such as the use of avatars, life in fanfics,[5] forums and the surrendering to the uninterrupted stream of varieties. Belonging to your time may require you to be connected 24 hours a day/7 days a week to a streaming news channel or to be part of *history* in real-time reactions to the big events on social networks. In the meantime, we have become voluntary and/or involuntary servants of the large internet companies, by using and accessing seemingly gratuitous services while wage labourers are fighting for the right and/or the obligation to disconnection (cf. Ribeiro 2018; Cardoso 2016; Fuchs-Eran 2012).

It is not only in the English language that we see the concept of update as a symptom of a reality or situation that continually increases and gains adherence. In Figure 5 the evolution of the word *actualización* in the database of books in Spanish indicates similar movement that can also be observed for the Italian *aggiornamento* or the French *mise à jour*.

Although the Google Ngram feature is not yet available for the Portuguese language, this absence may be partially replaced by a survey in the Digital Newspaper Library of the National Library of Rio de Janeiro. On this basis there are hundreds of newspapers and other serial publications that circulated in Brazil between the nineteenth and twentieth centuries. The comparison of the evolution of the terms '*progresso*' (progress), '*atualização*' (updating), '*atualizar*' (to update) and '*modernizar*' (to modernize) is shown in Figure 6,[6] elaborated from this newspaper library.

As, on the basis of Ngram, we can identify analogous phenomena, the growth of the semantic field around the word 'update' and the loss of energy of words like 'progress' in similar proportion, which may indicate some competitive relations between the two fields. Futurism in the first decades of the postwar period, so much in the grip of optimistic progress, seems to give way to the ideal of an updatist present-centred.

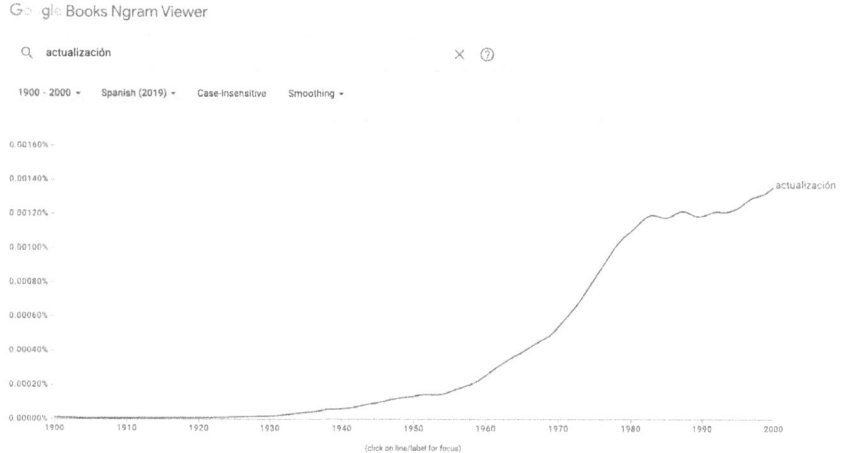

Figure 5 Frequency of the word *actualización* in the Spanish/2019 language base of Google Ngram. *Source*: Google Ngram, accessed on 19 July 2018.

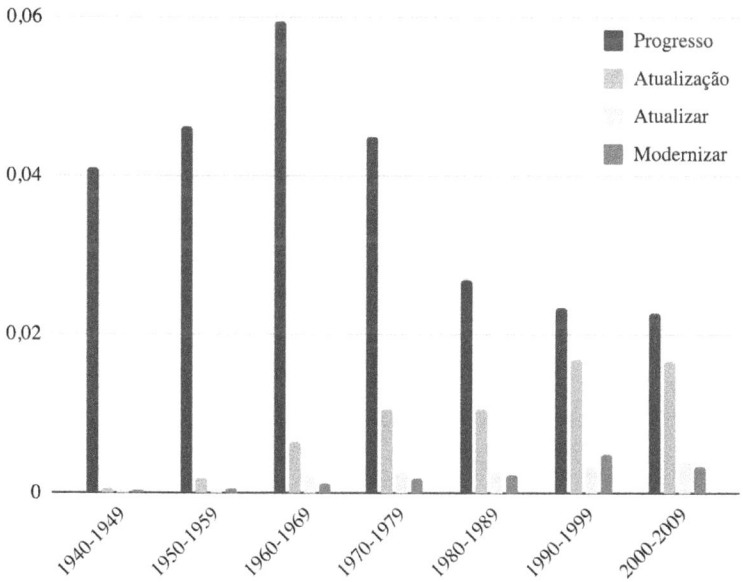

Figure 6 Evolution of the terms 'progress', 'updating', 'to update' and 'to modernize' in Portuguese at the Digital Newspapers Library of the National Library – RJ. *Source*: The authors.

In our reflection, the word 'updatism' helps to understand the persistence of certain levels of acceleration, dispersion and temporal dissociation, despite the crisis or closure of the future. We call the specific ways of connecting past-present-future as *temporalization of time*. In this direction, the emergence of the word 'update' as a concept of social-political relevance can be taken as a revealing phenomenon of new forms of temporalization. Seen as a metaphor for certain contemporary situations and experiences, the word can be helpful in understanding transformations in the lifeworlds. It can also be taken as a symptom of how time temporalizes in the current world and how the sensation of acceleration and multiplication of occurrences can be disconnected from decision, utopia and a totalizing and guiding notion of progress.

Thus, our bet is that some fragments of modern and contemporary timing can be approached around the category *updatism*, since we share the theoretical and methodological principle that there is a constant interrelation between concept and experience (cf., among others, Koselleck 2006; Araujo 2008; Bentivoglio 2010). Given the exploratory and initial character of our investigation, we intend to maintain a theoretical and methodological stance open to the dialogue between theory and empiricism. In this direction, we will consider, from the tradition already established in intellectual history (cf., e.g., Palti 1998; Avelar, Faria and Pereira 2012), the emergence of the word 'update' as an event, which means to consider it in its moment of enunciation as a sufficient and revealing structure of discursive achievements. As a historical testimony, this word gives us privileged access to the ways in which certain aspects of current life social experiences, conceives and prefigures reality. Such understanding involves analysing statements to capture several layers of a text and discourse, their uses and appropriations (cf., also, Certeau 2008). The understanding of the *meaning* of a statement does not focus only on *what has been said* (semantic content of statements), but especially: 'who said', 'how it was said', 'where it was said', 'to whom it was said', 'in what circumstances it was said'.

From this perspective, the fragments analysed here are taken as scales. For Paul Ricoeur (2007), the play of scales indicates an escape to the false alternative that structured the historical work between the partisans of the event and those of the long duration. At each scale, one observes aspects that are not seen in another and each view has its own legitimacy. The exercise of plays of scale is above all an exercise in methodological freedom. The principle of variation (cf. Revel 1998, 2010) opens up possibilities to articulate dynamically: updatism and theory (Chapter 1), updatism and historicism (Chapter 2) and updatism and current time (*atualidade*) (Chapters 3 and 4). Our fragments start from interaction logics in which different objects are constituted in relation to others. The choice of scales, the construction of contexts or the historicization of disputes, categories, concepts and facts invites us to come and go between phenomena and reflection. Such a challenge is induced both by us and by the phenomena (cf. Werner and Zimmermann 2003). These and other perspectives in the history of historiography, theory of history and intellectual history were fundamental to describe, conceptualize and interpret our historical time.

In the end, this book, less than the specular representation of a standstill reality, is an attempt at transformative intervention over realities with which we can relate only through fragments.

Notes

1 On the cautions and potentialities of using this instrument, see Pereira, Santos and Nicodemo 2015. On the use of the word 'actualism' in geology and philosophy, cf., among others, Faria 2014 and Menzel 2014.

2 Talking about the dissemination of this culture, especially associated to internet diffusion, Castels (2013) states, 'The Internet is not really a new technology: its ancestor, Arpanet, was first deployed in 1969 (Abbate 1999). But it was in the 1990s, when it was privatized and released from the control of the US Department of Commerce, that it spread worldwide at an extraordinary speed: in 1996 the first survey of Internet users counted about 40 million; in 2013 there are more than 2.5 billion, with China accounting for the largest number of Internet users. Moreover, for some time the spread of the Internet was limited by the difficulty of distributing terrestrial telecommunications infrastructure in developing countries. This has changed with the explosion of wireless communication in the early 21st century. In fact, in 1991, there were about 16 million wireless subscribers worldwide, by 2013 they are close to 7 billion (on a planet of 7.7 billion humans). Taking into account the family and community uses of mobile phones, and taking into account the limited use of these devices among children under five, we can say that humanity is almost totally connected, although with great levels of inequality in bandwidth as well as in the efficiency and price of the service.'

3 Since the first portuguese edition of this book, we have seen several references to its reception, as well as some spontaneous and alternative uses. In a blog post dated August 2018, we came across the following passage: 'What I like about the whole sparking joy thing is the acknowledgement that our attachment to stuff

isn't purely rational. What I don't like is some of the practices I've seen it lead to – what I categorise as rampant updatism. Like getting rid of all your towels, which, until yesterday, were perfectly functional, but now no longer spark joy and must be immediately updated to something more joy sparking'. https:// moretimethanmoney.co.nz/for-me-right-now-july/ accessed on 4 April 2023.

4 *The American Heritage Dictionary of the English Language*, Fifth Edition. Houghton Mifflin Harcourt Publishing Company, 2018.

5 One can catch a glimpse of the complexity of this new genre at https://en .wikipedia.org/wiki/Fanfic, accessed 25 September 2018, in addition to the growing academic literature on the phenomenon.

6 The values obtained in Figure 6 correspond to the frequency division of each word and the number of base pages in each decade. This procedure allowed us to normalize the relative meaning of each frequency value in the respective decade.

Updatism and theory

1.1. Temporality in the postmodern condition: Jean-François Lyotard

Although in his famous 1979 book, *The Postmodern Condition*, Lyotard does not directly address the problem of temporality, the book is still central to this debate for two reasons: its impact on the generation of thinkers who will face the theme in the following decades (Sim 2001; Malpas 2003; Marques 2017); and the clues that it gives us, in its precise diagnosis, about the effects of the post-industrial turnaround.

Gumbrecht does not hide the importance of Lyotard in his reflection, and of the general impact of Niklas Luhmann's systems theory: 'At the time, lived, thought and wrote in Paris thinkers of a truly world-wide fame: the philosophers Gilles Deleuze, Jacques Derrida and Jean-François Lyotard' (Gumbrecht 2015, p. 93).[1]

According to Wilmar Barbosa, who wrote the preface to the Brazilian edition, Lyotard would have abandoned utopia, being more 'concerned with the present and with the reinforcement of the criterion of performance – technological criterion – and thus he was aiming at strengthening "reality"' (Barbosa in Lyotard 2009, p. XIII). In spite of defining postmodernity as a 'cultural' phenomenon, as 'incredulity in the metanarratives', Lyotard does not analyse the impacts of this disbelief on the experience of historical time, although he points out several other related social phenomena that today appear as naturalized in our everyday life.

It is not that Lyotard did not have important sources for thinking about the temporal effects of the postmodern condition, since, almost ten years earlier, in 1967, one of the most important books of the Situationist Movement in France was published, *The Society of the Spectacle*, in which Guy Debord characterized late capitalism by the emptying of the authentic experience of objects, replaced by its spectacular mediated form. In his theses Debord speaks of a 'spectacular time', a 'strange present' in which 'the reality of time has been replaced by the publicity of time' and other valuable characterizations, but he does not even mention any variant of the word 'update'. By the end of the 1960s, the word might have been a too innovative approach to be used in the philosophical vocabulary of Debord's Marxism, although it seems evident to us that he perceived the emergence of this new dimension of the experience of historical time (Debord 2005, pp. 109–18).[2]

The crisis of authority of the specialists (experts) emphasized by Lyotard and the notion of consensus to the detriment of the inventors and their 'paralogies' are now widely explored by authors who analyse the positive and negative, utopic and dystopic impacts of the social networks, of the digital era and the post-human (cf. e.g. Berry 2011, p. 40; Braidotti 2015, p. 150). Of course the digital revolution meant the creation of other hero-experts, the programmers, but even they did not escape the threat of the obsolete, since 'it was not only the introduction of automatic programming that inspired the narratives of male expertise under attack, but also the introduction of – or rather the appreciation of – the (automatic) computer' (Chun 2011, p. 43). For Rigney, 'in a world where images and text can be copied so easily, the possibilities for interactivity are increased and the boundaries between production and reception, between expert and amateur, become much more diffuse' (Rigney 2010, p. 111).[3] A positive view of these transformations can be found in David Berry, who, studying the policies and practices of free software, believes that they can articulate 'productive forms of self-knowledge and discipline [. . .] uncoordinated and descentred models of creativity' (Berry 2008, p. x). He argues that 'this new form of code-humanism is a necessary political imaginary that will have huge consequences' (ibid., p. 197).

In Lyotard, the digitization of society would lead to knowledge having to be translated into amounts of information (Lyotard 2009, p. 4). The 'machine-interpreters', at that time exemplified by pocket translators of 'Craig and Lexicon companies' with 1,500-word memories, pointed to the leap that we would see with the development of Artificial Intelligence and Neural Networks, even if a great abyss seems to separate these early and modest attempts from what we find today in applications like Google Translator (Lewis-Kraus

2016). This abyss does not prevent the author from anticipating the forces that constitute our world today, like the transformation of knowledge and information into the great product of contemporary capitalism, distributed as streaming services. From the quotation from a study by J. M. Treille it is quite clear that as early as 1979, Lyotard had a precise vision of the reach of the digital revolution:

> Not enough has been said about the new possibilities of dissemination of memory, particularly thanks to semiconductors and lasers [. . .]. Anyone will soon be able to store at a low price the information wherever he/she wants, and, further, will be able to process it autonomously. (Lyotard 2009, p. 8)

Analysing what he calls the 'ideology of transparency' and its impacts on the legitimacy of the State and Liberalism, Lyotard described 'parallel flows of knowledge' that would navigate on the same channels as financial flows: 'but some of which will be reserved for the "decision makers", while the others will serve to pay each person's perpetual debt with respect to the social bond' (Lyotard 2009, p. 7).[4]

A gloomy view of global capitalism is emerging throughout his book. In his reading of Luhmann, it became evident that the emancipation narrative was merely a peripheral compensation of the social system in a description that could be taken as defining what we are calling updatism:

> the harmony between the need and the hopes of individuals and groups with the functions that ensure the system is nothing more than an annexed component of its functioning; the true goal of the system, what makes it program itself as an intelligent machine, is the optimization of the global relation between its input and output, that is, its performativity [. . .] being entropy the only alternative to this improvement of performances, that is, the decline. (Lyotard 2009, p. 21)

The metaphors of the digital world and the perspective of an automated system of governance, completely detached from external ends, are aspects that help us understand the apocalyptic and gloomy atmosphere, or even cynical resignation, that will take over from part of this generation.[5] The loss of the social value of historical traditions, of identifications with the class, with the nation and with the profession, frees the digital man from the supposedly emancipatory agendas of modernity.

The purpose and individual orientation seem to be steadily falling back into the personal sphere. Citing, in a note, an analysis by J. Bouveresse of *The Man Without Qualities*, Lyotard transcribes:

> Considering in particular the state of science, a man is made only of what people say he is or of what is done with what he is [. . .] The world is one in which lived events become independent of man . . . It is a world of the future, the world of what happens without its affecting anyone, and without anyone's being responsible. (Lyotard 2009, p. 33)

In this passage we can anticipate the consequences of this description for the experience of historical time. This world of the future will be more and more our current world and, for obvious reasons, we are losing the ability to talk about the future with the same resourcefulness as Lyotard. Gumbrecht's generation was the first to diagnose this situation with clarity, that is, this future without qualities which makes predictions and diagnoses of modern type impossible or irrelevant. Like Chateaubriand, as we shall see in Chapter 2, the Lyotard of 1979 is a man who lives in the confluence and in the mixture of experiential content when the forms of culture explode. It is still capable of producing modern diagnoses, but the world that emerges from these predictions makes this gesture impossible or obsolete. The nostalgia of the modern intellectual that is becoming a constant in the humanities courses seems to be one more document of this situation.

In this horizon of metanarrative crisis, Lyotard includes nation-states, political parties, professional identities and historical traditions. Unbelieved and freed from these bonds, subjectivities would not be isolated but arranged 'in a texture of relationships', 'placed on the "nodes" of communication circuits', what we would today call networks. Lyotard does not hide his optimism for the possibilities of this new arrangement (Lyotard 2009, pp. 27–8).

But it is in the description of narrative knowledge that we can find the elements to think of temporality in *The Postmodern Condition*. For the author, the narrative time is of a double nature, organized by meter and accent. While the meter is the regular division of temporal flux, the accent is the gesture of shortening or extending these spaces producing rhythm. In mythical narratives there would be the predominance of the meter over the accent; in this case, 'time ceases to be the medium of memorization and becomes an immemorial cadence which, in the absence of observable differences between

periods, prevents them from enumerating them and relegates them to oblivion'
(Lyotard 2009, p. 40).

A society in which reporting is the 'key form of competence' could detach
itself from the need to remember the past, since

> [the society] finds the matter of its social bond not only in the meaning of
> the narratives it tells but in the act of reciting them. The narrative's reference
> may seem to belong to the past, but in reality it is always contemporary
> with this act. It is the present act that unfolds, each time, the ephemeral
> temporality that stretches between the 'I have heard' and 'you will hear'.
> (Lyotard 2009, p. 41)

Lyotard is describing 'non-Western societies', which would question the
legitimacy and providing conditions of what is stated in the narrative.
Narratives are not produced by subjects who need to answer for the cognitive
value of their positions; the narrator only executes the story producing
an evanescent and immemorial time. Considering that the book's thesis
affirms that in post-industrial societies we would be experiencing a kind
of abandonment and corrosion of the traditional narratives of legitimacy,
emancipation and speculation, based on strongly accentuated reports, it would
not be unreasonable to think that postmodern temporality would be closer to
this 'evanescent' time. However, these connections are not developed. In 1979,
Lyotard prophesied that databases would be 'the "nature" for postmodern
man' (p. 93). Today social networks like Facebook, Twitter and Instagram
are the environments in which the mutations of this new nature happen; the
very image of a database seems ancient, it being more common today for us
to speak of streams and continuous and decentralized circulation. In these
environments, the value of the story seems to be more in its flow, a kind of
melopedia in which we seek definitive accents in vain or where the continuous
dispute by accent becomes the meter.

What allows the accent to produce the memorizing effect is precisely
its ability to interrupt the meter, to change it. In the continuous stream of
news that we deliver ourselves today in social networks, this interruption is
impossible, and the technological acceleration made routine seems to lose its
ability to accentuate the stories. If everything changes very quickly, but without
breaking expectations, if change itself becomes the expectation, can time slow
down and approach a new type of immemorial time: the updatism?

1.2. Hans-Ulrich Gumbrecht: Updatism as a broad present

In his most ambitious book, in theoretical terms, *Production of Presence* (2003), Gumbrecht (2010) responds to this picture of crisis described and anticipated by Lyotard in 1979. For both, the problem seems to be how to guarantee a survival for the Humanities in *The Postmodern Condition*. However, Gumbrecht oscillates between a weak optimism with the loss of grand narratives and a pessimism with the perception that this loss may have been the result not of exhaustion but of the deepening of the culture of meaning in the digital age. Against his own desire to establish a liberating rupture of our time from 'modernity', Gumbrecht's account also opens the possibility of the opposite interpretation. His description of the desire for presentification as a symptom of our time can illustrate the agony of practices of presence rather than its reactive or compensatory generalization (Gumbrecht 2014).[6]

Six years after the first German edition of *Production of Presence*, in the book *Our Broad Present*, Gumbrecht (2014, 2015) analyses the relations between digital technologies and temporalizations. In the essay 'Infinite Availability: About Hypercommunication (and Old Age)', his perspective is predominantly pessimistic without, however, failing to point out opportunities or gaps in the new situation and celebrating what he considers to be an exhaustion of modernity. By making everything and everyone available, information technology risks destroying the conditions for thinking, which would depend on a swing between 'presence' and 'meaning'. While Hartog (2003) and other authors who before him have stressed a supposed end or exhaustion of modernity lament the loss of an open future, of utopia, of historical sense, Gumbrecht sees in these same diagnoses ambivalent possibilities for the deepening of a culture of the body and of the presence, in a reflexive lineage closer to authors like Lyotard and Luhmann.

In the beginning of this essay, Gumbrecht claims to be among those who feel displaced in the digital environment. He resisted as much as he could the technological innovations and sought to defend his choice with a rigorous discipline that would limit his use of resources such as email. The story begins to interest us with the event of an 'automatic updating' (*automatic upgrading* [*sic*])[7] of the software of his work computer that would have shared his email box with his home computer, one of the effects and possibilities of cloud computing.

Even acknowledging the democratic character and the positive side of this new availability, the emphasis given by Gumbrecht, like other analysts of the same phenomenon (Gumbrecht 2006), lies in the ambivalent reciprocity of the process: being online means being able to dispose of the other at any moment but also to be increasingly available to others. Gumbrecht does not deny the somewhat luddite nature of his resistance, nor the prejudice that giving himself over to these new resources would lead him to a certain intellectual decay. Although he does not explain the nostalgic aspect of his posture, it is evident that this aspect is present to some degree.[8] This image of a kind of decay, even if not deepened, is reinforced by some examples of the side effects of using email and social networks that, in 2010, when the original edition was launched, weren't so obvious.

On this point, in dialogue with Gumbrecht, Oliveira (2015a) states that for the native digital generation, there were no adaptation strategies like those described previously. Thus, new behaviours are stimulated, such as the compulsive **Binge-watching phenomenon:**

> the great reduction of the weight of the end to the course of history, produces a temporality that is both pleasurable and repetitive . . . The new habit transmutes the fear of obsolescence that accompanies the tireless effort to adapt to new technologies. (Oliveira 2015a, p. 312)

The first formulation in which Gumbrecht elaborates the idea of nostalgia draws attention to a certain compromise, a certainly very personal ethic of not letting objects and situations with which he grew up and which would constitute his 'being-in-the-world' disappear, threatened by the latest evolutionary deeds.[9] In a context where pressure for a continuous and accelerated technological development is identified, in which the availability of everything, including of ourselves for others and the technological processes is extended, Gumbrecht affirms the hope that some objects and situations with which he got used to continue to exist for some time. This decision to fight against the obsolescence of certain objects and habits would function as a non-compensatory resistance to technological acceleration, since it would not be a matter of moving the value of these objects to their non-pragmatic aspect, as in the museographic historicization.

Gumbrecht seems to shift some of the energy from the adaptive effort to the maintenance of certain obsolete objects and habits. In one of his many trips to the city of Mariana (Brazil), it was very difficult to convince him that it was not necessary to mail to his office in Stanford two mini cassette tapes of the analog recorder, which was still his work tool. He was unwilling to allow them to be scanned and sent to his secretary by email. Some disgust or fear of altering an aspect of his work and life routine was evident. He struggled to keep an object that should be in the trash, in a museum, or in a shop for lovers of vintage products.

In a tone of confession, a trace of his prose, Gumbrecht recognizes that his resistance to technological innovation may be due to the fear of not being able to use it with the excellence he expects of his intellectual performance, of a graceful and natural behaviour that can only be acquired with dedication, effort and repetition. In giving the example of passengers of an airplane who, after being a short time without connection during the flight, anxiously connect their cell phones as soon the aircraft reaches the ground, in the hypothetical example, to announce to those who were waiting at the airport for their arrival, he denounces the drive for total availability.

The author perceives the emptying of physical presence by the dilution of the ubiquitous virtual presence. Here we have an important point in his diagnosis of what we are calling updatism: in his typology 'culture of presence' versus 'culture of meaning', updatism would be the hypertrophy of meaning. What we can question is: What is the place for a non-historicist chronotope in an increasingly historicist world? Does the force of presence as compensatory energy for meaning justify speaking of a new chronotope? Is not his desire to bid farewell to modernity a sort of reactive fantasy, in line with the aforementioned Oliveira? His evidently anti-modern discourse would not be without place in a world that is not the end of modernity but its most extreme development. To retake his argument in the text 'Waterfalls of Modernity' (1998), it would be as if the fourth and last cascade were not to undo the others, but the non-progressive accumulation of yet another wave of modernization.[10] We left open, however, if the extension of the analogy would not be pointing to another gesture of resistance than a simple compensation.

The author also gives the example of invitations to lectures, in which requests are made for previous versions of the text, authorization for video recording and digital propagation on the internet. This excess of registers would deprive the character of the event of being in a lecture. 'Nothing is really new, nothing is lost . . . ' (2014, L. 1502). Can we take Gumbrecht's descriptions as symptoms of updatism? In this culture of continuous variety we may wonder if there would still be room for 'differences' in a history that accelerates and is hungry for new 'events'. Can nothing different really happen?

Gumbrecht refuses the idea that an electronic debate can actually generate intellectual intensity, even claiming that electronic discussions produce, at best, 'spiritual mediocrity'. Can we agree to such a definitive judgement? Would not this severe judgement come, in part, from his own inability, confessed lack of grace, to deal with these new media? If the digitization is an extension of the properly modern form, it must be able to produce some intellectual intensity, even if it is not intensity of presence. Maybe for Gumbrecht the words 'intensity' and 'meaning' are incompatible, but are they really?

This doubt seems to feed his ambivalence about the characterization of the present age by the emergence of a new chronotope and the extreme realization of modern times, as is evident in this passage:

> This is the reason why the electronic based hypercommunication brings to its unsurpassed conclusion the process of modernity, as the process in which the human subject as pure consciousness emancipated itself and triumphed over the human body. (L. 1541)

In this passage, he clearly states that electronic communication would complete modernity as disembodiment, a world as pure mind, a theme that has been developing since its programmatic formulation of a non-hermeneutic field in the 1980s (Gumbrecht1998, 2006).[11] But how to think of a new chronotope in this scenario? What evidence would we have of a possible overcoming or undoing of the modern chronotope? The main evidence pointed out would be a general sense of slowdown of time, which would nullify various aspects of modernity as formulated, in particular, in Koselleck`s description (cf. Gumbrecht 2012).

However, soon after, Gumbrecht insists that a sensual perception will always resist a conceptual reduction and that the digital present is marked by the possibility of complex temporal simultaneities. This digital simultaneity that seems to distance itself from the idea of a linear and empty time of historicist 'progress' is breaking or deepening modernity? This new cascade of modernity, which would not undo all aspects of the others (cf. Gumbrecht 1998), could be seen as a way of deepening and mutating more structural tendencies of the modern time. Leaving aside or transforming what in historicism may now appear as not fundamental, the idea of progress and formation is replaced by the continuous and accelerated updating of the Same: updatism. As the brief foray into the history of the word 'update' seems to reveal, it absorbs part of the semantic charge of the concept of progress, a phenomenon that seems to have been photographed in the Google Books database, as we showed in the introduction to this book.

According to Gumbrecht, 'in today's electronic present, there is nothing "of the past" that we need to leave behind, or anything "of the future" that cannot be made present by a simulated anticipation' (L. 1559). The conjunction of this past that does not pass with anticipations would form a broad and slow 'present'. But the author himself keeps the question open: 'But I am fully aware that this is just another revolution of the Gray Panthers' (L. 1563). The 'Gray Panther' revolution alludes to the rights movement of aging created in 1970 by the American activist Margareth Kuhn (Maggie Kuhn). Refusing to accept compulsory retirement at age 65, Kuhn began the movement that questioned the elderly's place in society, a struggle against obsolescence that, in a way, can reverse and extend the sense and the duration of the current. We shall return to the 1970s and its forms of updating.[12]

Therefore, the present as a brief transition moment, typical of historicism, would be replaced by the complex simultaneities of the digital universe. The argument depends on our agreement with two statements: (1) That this notion of fleeting present has really been hegemonic in historicism. (2) That, by the current deceleration, it would be replaced by complex simultaneities. However, perhaps this present as a simple moment of transition has not been so hegemonic and we could identify other forms of temporalization of the present in the historicist chronotope, as we intend to show in the next chapter. Besides the differences of rhythm, there is a reproduction and permanence of the present that can be identified even in the historicist heyday. Although threatened by a virtually superior future, historicism produced the acute awareness of the present as the best of times, the one that reveals and realizes the historical meaning. As for the second statement, current simultaneities seem to be largely improper (see Section 1.4), having little to do with the instant and now, thematized by authors like Benjamin and Heidegger as the counterpoint to the empty and successive time of historicism or of the everyday life.

In our formulation, updatism is experienced as the quasi-magical belief in the reproduction of reality. Shortly after having written the first version of this section, in 2016 we experienced a substantial loss of research records when a new version of Windows was automatically updated. Although a substantive part of the material was in the cloud, some files were saved on the desktop of a laptop. The Windows update simply erased all material that was saved on the desktop. In a society that increasingly believes in the unavoidable need for updates, which are embedded in the very media of communication, such an event has the potential to reveal the weaknesses of a system that is at all times experienced as a guarantee and guaranteed. The more reliant we are on digital storage and its updating, the more we run the risk of a catastrophic loss, or a catastrophic leak like invasions of privacy. What we call updatism seems to depend on our belief that somewhere there is a force, a system, which is even incomprehensible to the vast majority of people, perhaps even to all, but which still guarantees the stability of our world. As recorded in one of the forums we have consulted in the vain hope of solving the problem with the Windows update, the predominant climate is a sense of despair, the catastrophic loss of hope, the difficulty of believing that in times of total availability something may simply disappear.

We are convinced that not updating involves several risks: your antivirus may not be up to new hackers, your bank account may become insecure, your photos, organized and stored in clouds, can be exploited by governments, companies and individuals, as one of the editors of the 'Oficina do Net' page raises the alarm in the post 'The risks of not updating software'.[13]

There is broad room for a phenomenology of updatism that could describe these new phenomena and devices. The jump to cloud computing radicalized one of the most perverse features of capitalist society. The obsolescence of the object becomes the obsolescence of the real itself, completely transformed into the product of human action and, therefore, in constant need of updating. Streaming services funded by monthly payments make it clear that either the consumer pays regularly for access to the up-to-date digital reality or he/she is relegated to an underworld that is anachronistic, insecure, dangerous and full of risks. One aspect that could be developed from Gumbrecht's account would be the right to obsolescence as a socially available alternative, not only a personal or class privilege.

1.3. Updatism and presentism: The narrative of François Hartog

Fixing the gaze on what has supposedly gone or disappeared may prevent us from seeing the reconfigurations and displacements (Zawdzki 2008). As we intend to show, we believe that this seems to be the case with François Hartog's diagnosis.

In the preface to the 2012 French edition of *Regimes of Historicity: Presentism and Time Experiences*, Hartog defines presentism, as he had already done in the first edition of 2003, as an experience of time in which the present imposes itself as the only horizon. We would live in a world of the tyranny of the present omnipotent, omnipresent and hypertrophied: 'unique present: this of the tyranny of the instant and the marasmus of a perpetual present' (Hartog 2012, p. 6; Pereira and Mata 2013).

In *Croire en l'histoire* (2013), Hartog maintains the same criticism when he states that presentism is 'the closing of the future and the growth of an omnipresent present' (Hartog 2013, p. 30); and 'the future, in the end, has become a burden that people, companies or institutions no longer want to carry. [. . .] And for the past there is memory (with patrimony and commemoration) and justice' (Hartog 2013, p. 103). We would live through crises replaced by every new scandal. We would be focused on immediate responses to the immediate (as in the episode 'National Anthem', from the Black Mirror series, in which the British Prime Minister is forced to have live sex with a pig as demanded by the hijackers of one of the princesses of the royal family).[14] There would be a social and historiographical passage 'of long duration to everything is an event' (2013, pp. 263–6). Presentism would be the time in which there is nothing but the event. For the author, for example, from 11 September 2001 onwards, the American administration would have decided to found a ground zero in world history. The war on terrorism would be a new and unique present. For Hartog, the attack showed the logic of the contemporary event: it comes to be seen as it happens, it historicizes and 'brings in itself its own celebration: under the eyes of the cameras. And in this sense it is absolutely presentist' (Hartog 2003, p. 156). After all, the real-time cameras on the second aircraft would have created the conditions for this. Similarly, the same would have occurred in 1968 and 1989, with the Student Revolts and the fall of the Berlin Wall.

In a 2015 interview, the author reflects on the relationship between computing, crisis of history and new experience of time. For him, the informatics revolution reinforces the rupture: 'the real time of the market is presentist, it is as much of the order of the microsecond as it is continuous. A whole economy of the moment is put into action: the financial, the media, the politics, the social and also the social networks' (Hartog 2015, p. 283).

However, the French historian points out that this new regime is not univocal, there would be several layers of presentism: 'There is the presentism of circulation, of fluxes, of permanent acceleration, of deterritorialization, of markets and of the digital economy' (Hartog 2015, p. 284). In this context, the past is constantly fabricated for the present, especially through images, films, series, plays and scenarios, and history discipline does not know what to say, for its authority over the past has been superseded.[15] History discipline presents serious difficulties in 'apprehending the world in its current course. The modern concept of history is basically futuristic and, from the moment the present imposes itself as a dominant category, history also does not see it clearly' (Hartog 2015, p. 286).

Hartog emphasizes that the notion and 'valuation' of the heritage must be seen from the present, in an ambiguous game with the temporalities and rhythms of the market, especially with the tourism industry. From the 1960s the faith in progress was replaced by the concern to preserve. One of the signs of this process is the commercialization and instantaneous museification of the remains of the Berlin Wall shortly after its fall. In more recent reflections the relationship between memory and/or patrimony with presentism was slightly complexified by the author, for the place of memory in the contemporary world can be at the same time symptom and possibility of cure:

> But it [the memory] is also what makes the thing complex, this phenomenon that allows, in a certain sense, to escape the presentism by reason of certain convocation of the past. But under a mode of memory or what we call memory, because in reality, in many cases it is not about memory. It is about the reconstruction of something that, in fact, one does not have access. We can see this throughout the debate around the memory of slavery. Even in Brazil, where slavery was abolished too late, what does the memory of slavery mean? Then memory is a presentist, but also an attempt to escape presentism, and in any case, at the same time, it must be placed in relation to a loss, if I take my vocabulary, of the evidence of history. (Hartog 2012a, p. 367)

Four words, in particular, gravitate around presentism and even translate themselves into politics: memory, patrimony, celebration and identity. But, also, of concepts, according to Hartog, detemporalized, like modernity, postmodernity and globalization. Given its futuristic dimension, the modern concept of history no longer works to grasp the future of societies and guide men in the present. In other words, history and historiography (reality as a temporal process and discipline) have lost their efficacy in the face of a catastrophic future and the crisis of discipline authority, two phenomena that feed back to each other.[16]

A future that is no longer indefinitely open, but increasingly constrained, if not closed, because the most remarkable change of the last thirty years would have been what it calls the retreat of the future. The hypothesis of the new experience of time (sometimes taken as evidence) cannot be understood, according to the author, on the record of nostalgia (a regime better than another) or of denunciation. In the preface already quoted, Hartog states that in the book, the question had not been asked whether we would live in a full or provisional presence (*par défaut*). Given the impossibility of a past return ('where the past commands') could we think that we are living only a suspension, a stop, so that the future takes control over again? Or is it an unprecedented experience of time? In this direction, Hartog affirms that the current preference for memory at the expense of historiography is consistent with the present experience of time, in which the present either is abolished at the instant or seems perpetual.[17]

In front of the sketched picture, it would be left to the historian to offer to the societies one of his/her attributes: the distanced look. The instrumentality provided by the notion of regimes of historicity would help to create the necessary distance to see better. The hypothesis (the presentism) and the instrument (the regime of historicity) would complement each other. One question that arises from this position is: doesn't this apology of the distanced look consist in retrieving one of the great ingenuities of historicism? After all, is distance production not really a game in the present of the historian between closeness and detachment?

The regime of historicity is understood as articulation between past, present and future or a mixed constitution of the three categories – with one of the elements being dominant – throughout the human experience of time. Why and how this predominance should take place is not clear in his argumentation, in view of the theoretical foundations of its conception of historical time, centred on a fragmentary and partial use of the Koselleckian description of modernity. In any case, Hartog points out that 'regime of historicity' and 'presentism' are not realities but analytical categories, ideal types constructed by the historian, without mechanical successions and without coinciding with a substantive concept of the epoch. Throughout the 2003 book, however, these categories are used beyond their heuristic functions, in particular the notion of presentism, of a judgement, of a positioning, about the contemporary experience of time (Delacroix 2009). The idea of a heuristic procedure sometimes justifies the lack of theoretical and empirical foundation of some arguments and conclusions, or of a more focused reflection on its basic phenomenon, the orders of time.

Given how the category is effectively used throughout the main book (*Regimes of Historicity*, 2003), it is hard to agree that it does not assume the function of a substantive description of historical epochs. Moreover, the French historian relies on meta-historical categories such as experience and expectation that remain theoretically undeveloped throughout his argument. The category presentism allows him to speak in a global perspective on the entire twentieth century with a very limited and homogeneous amount of evidence and proof. An example: 'the twentieth century has allied, finally, futurism and presentism. If it was initially more futuristic than presentist, it ended up more presentist than futurist' (Hartog 2003, p. 119). But in his defence, it could be observed that this type of procedure is common currency in much of modern Western historiography.

We would like to present some criticisms and developments elaborated and/or systematized by two Brazilian historians. Fernando Nicolazzi points out that some readers indicate, in Hartog, an interpretation marked by nostalgia, melancholy, by pessimism and scepticism, especially in the face of the future already defined as gloomy. Moreover, 'the mutual references between historicity and historiography are questioned, after all, a regime of historicity may have different forms of historical writing' (Nicolazzi 2010, p. 251; Nicolazzi 2017; Blocker and Haddad 2006). Another aspect that draws the attention of some critics is the way in which the author constructs quick passages between 'cases' and the individual scales to more collective, global and societal dimensions of the experience of the time. This generalization abolishes a certain plurality and subaltern/alternative experiences of time, despite the openness that Hartog's essay format offers us as a remedy, in the double meaning of the term, to face such questions. But we know that the essay form may also mask the exercise of a sort of epistemic privilege, which authorizes speaking out and is oblivious to conventions.

More or less in the same direction, Faria (2014, p. 403) states: 'one does not start from the thesis that we live in a presentist age, or at a time when the social experience of time has been spatialized or liquidated in any way', quoting Peter Pal Pelbart's *O tempo não-reconciliado (Unconciled Time)*. Faria denounces the paradoxical homogenization of time still inherent in this procedure: 'the image of the past as a present to be revisited implies an operation that tends to cancel the difference, the plurality of times' (2014, p. 403). The irreversibility of time that has passed should not be taken as absolute, since 'the past also returns, either as memory, trauma or repetition, and so it continues to operate in the current time [*atualidade*]' (2014, p. 403).

João Paulo Pimenta (2015), in turn, highlights what he calls conceptual imprecision, in particular, of Hartog's use of the categories of historicity and presentism as a description-signification of realities without proper reasoning. For the author, the differences between the proposals of Koselleck and Hartog are not clarified, especially because the French historian neglects a central aspect in the koselleckian theory of modernity related to presentism, namely, the progressive acceleration of historical time.[18] In this perspective, the author asks whether the French historian escaped the tendency of 'our times' to 'overestimate the observable present, resulting in an overvaluation of the presentism of a present that may not be so distinct from that created by modernity for some time ago, and still re-created by it' (Pimenta 2015, p. 404).

As we will show later on, this simplification, at many moments justified by Hartog, when he refuses, for example, to assume the differences between theoretical and historiographic work, produces innumerable tensions between what the author claims to do and what his book effectively produces. We know, for example, that affirming the formal aspect of certain analytical categories, either as ideal types or heuristic instruments, should not serve as a safe conduct for much more ambitious affirmations and historical descriptions. Such descriptions need to be confronted with their theoretical, epistemological and ontological assumptions. Thus, one of the most problematic aspects is the absence of a theory of historical time that could remove from the analysis a certain impressionism that tends at all times to unmediated causal explanations or chains, as if time could be taken as a kind of hidden subject of the phenomena, or even more often, reduced to the symptom of historical events and processes. Temporality, in Hartog, sometimes appears as a by-product of the forms in which, for example, ancients, moderns and savages are articulated. Therefore, little is said of the theoretical-methodological conditions for its observation, something that, in *Begriffsgeschichte*'s theory, depends on a long discussion about historical concepts and their dual nature of fact and indicator.

In few words, temporality often appears in Hartog only as an indicator of phenomena that are apparently external and determinant to them. As we shall attempt to show from Heidegger's analysis, we believe that part of the inadequacies of the notion of presentism may be the result of a one-dimensional conception of what is present.[19]

1.4. Heidegger and the temporalizations of the present

Paul Ricoeur (2012) points out that 'Augustine and Heidegger are, at least for me, the only thinkers who have taken the dialectic of the past, the present, and the future as the principal theme of their conception of time' (p. 338). And especially,

> as for Heidegger, it seems evident that the problem of differentiation of the three instances of time is established from its presumed unity. [. . .] Thus, it is located, beyond the question of pluralization, and also of dispersion of the three instances, that of its articulation. (p. 339)

Ricouer (2012) stresses the importance of Heidegger's gesture in differentiating past and having-been; our bet is that we can extend this understanding to the dimension of the present. Although less evident, in *Being and Time*, the present, as we pretend to show, also has different dimensions and will also receive different nomenclatures.

Naturally, the use of elements of Heidegger's philosophy serves us here to point out how it still prefigures an important part of our philosophical diagnoses of the present time. The question of whether or not a significant part of his work is intrinsically linked to Heidegger's anti-Semitism becomes a more than urgent task (Mitchell and Trawny 2017), in the same line of efforts to demonstrate how Eurocentric racism also contextualizes our ways of feeling and thinking and much of the cultural legacy of the so-called West. Forgetting thinkers and their works, however comprehensible a moral reaction it may be, will not free us from their eventual effects, quite the opposite.

In Heidegger's case, accepting the 'contamination' of his critique of modernity by the deep prejudices of his time should not lead us to ignore that modernity, rooted in the metaphysical tradition or not, has brought with it enormous consequences and threats to what we can consider a sustainable human existence for all people and the planet. In any case, engagement with the vocabulary of Being and Time in the following paragraphs does not imply any kind of adherence to a supposed Heideggerian philosophical programme, if such a thing can arise from a consequent reading of his works.

In the fourth chapter of the second section of *Being and Time*, entitled 'Temporality and Everydayness', which is entirely dedicated to the analysis of the temporality of disclosedness (*erschlossenheit*), Heidegger (2003, pp. 324–59) addresses the everydayness of *Dasein*, starting from the temporal constitution of the existential structures of understanding, attunement (*befindlichkeit*), falling prey (*verfallen*) and discourse. These structures are understood as fundamental traits of what differentiates Dasein from all other beings: care (*sorge*), that is, his being always in relation to another Dasein.[20] Despite the tendency to understand these categories as individual, in the economy of *Being and Time* they are ontic-ontological, that is, constituents of any and all humans. Thus, although the phenomenological description departs from aspects of the everyday world, leading an unaware reader to imagine that Heidegger was dealing with individual subjects, the conclusions, at least if we accept the author's assumptions, are of general validity, making no sense, for example, the individual-society opposition that some critics have traditionally claimed (cf. Ricoeur 1997; Ankersmit 2012). The existential description-analysis of human is not the description of traces of concrete individuals that only then would be universalized by abstraction.

Although it bears specific temporalizations, it is in the set of relations between understanding, attunement, falling prey and discourse that Heidegger asserts that we can find the structural unity of temporality of care as the key to the temporality of Dasein. What we want to understand in what follows is the multiplicity of past, present and future dimensions in these structures. A big part of the literature on historicity has treated the present as a singular and self-evident reality. We will see that we can address it in another way, revealing its diverse possibilities for the understanding of the temporalizations.

We have no room here to analyse each of the four structures mentioned by Heidegger. We know that in his analysis each of the three temporal dimensions is attributed in a particular way to an existential structure, being the discourse of its revelation. The past would be especially attached to attunement, the future to understanding and the present to falling prey. Moreover, in each existential structure (attunement, understanding, falling prey) the three temporal dimensions (past, present, future) would be brought together in specific arrangements (ecstatic unity) in both 'authentic-proper' and 'inauthentic-improper' modes. We will deal with the three existentials that we consider emblematic and sufficient to direct our argument, namely: the temporality of understanding, centred in the future and particularly associated with authenticity; the temporality of falling prey, focused on the present and exemplary for the understanding of 'improper' modes; and the temporality of the attunement, particularly focused on the past.

The German words that Heidegger uses in the distinction between proper and improper are *eigentlich* and *uneigentlich*. The first form is a colloquial expression with the sense of really, truly, properly, etc. Historians should remember Ranke's famous phrase, '*wie es eigentlich gewesen*', in which the expression is translated as 'really'. In the philosophical translations of Heidegger's work, the most frequent is that the 'authentic-inauthentic' pair be used. We must take some precautions to not let ourselves be carried away by the face value of these words and to fall into the temptation of a Manichean opposition. In *Being and Time*, it is clear that Dasein is in most cases moving in the dimension of inauthenticity but that its most original condition occurs when it assumes in the disclosure and decides the previously given world as possibility, rather than a naturalized substance. Thus the phenomena that Dasein generally interprets as 'improperly' or 'inauthentic' are founded or can be better understood in the proper/authentic dimension. We cannot simply think that the difference between improper and proper is reduced to a polarity of the positive-negative type. Both dimensions are equally constitutive of the human; what Heidegger seeks to reveal are the consequences of these structures for our understanding of the world.

In Heidegger, the attunement appears as the first way that Dasein relates to the surrounding world; even before any understanding, interpretation or discourse, Dasein is in some affective disposition, tuned by some climate.[21] Specifically, the attunement is organized as a specific constellation of moods (*stimmungen*) such as fear, anguish, boredom, anger and so on. Thus, all understanding is acclimatized, consonant or attuned by a mood setting or disposition. Heidegger then asks about the temporal constitution of this connection between humour and understanding.[22]

The climate displaces the human from itself, allowing a disclosure to the existing environment, or the there of being-there (Dasein). As being-thrown into a world that precedes it, Dasein discloses itself to the past as the having-been, that is, the past that still acts. Moods like fear, anguish, sadness and happiness are the first openings between the Dasein and its there. Therefore, the temporal form of the having-being as an existential structure of the human is at the basis of the attunement. The other temporal ecstases, future and present, are then modified, as we shall see in the analysis of the temporality of understanding and falling prey.

Heidegger wants to demonstrate the temporal constitution of the ontological structure of the disposedness, that is, of the attunement, 'to make visible the temporality of humor' (1993, p. 138). By its primary temporalization in the past, mood has as its basic existential character a bringing back to. Thus, by constantly bringing back, mood reveals a way of the past as the having-been. In this world that exists before humans are thrown into it, mood is like a tiger's leap that opens up the human to the world: like the tiger that looks at the prey and, with that, awaits, and this awaiting holds in itself a return, a coming back, and generates an expectation.

Heidegger confines himself to describing the temporality of two humours he had already covered in the first section of the book: fear and anguish. Defined already in the first part as an improper mood, it becomes evident that in *fear* there is at stake a dimension of the future as awaiting. We always fear something that comes to us, the expectation of an approaching evil is one of the temporal structures of fear. But this threatening future, in the mood of fear, means not simply a fear of something to come but a fear for its own, a fear of harm in its own there. This future fear that threatens the there (established world) of being-there (human) in its occupations with things and caring for other people produces effects (affections) such as depression, distress, confusion and turmoil. In the *confusion* of fear we tend to *forget* our possibilities, reducing them to the more immediate there, which we imagine to be at risk. By confusing him or herself with his/her there, the human loses what is his/her own, that is, his/her potentiality of being. In this oblivion he or she then deals exclusively with the immediate, of what is at hand. In depression, being-there is related to its being-thrown, in the negative sense, closing itself to the future, waiting for it as an approaching evil, which again throws it towards the immediate in a search for protection: 'Taking care of things which fears for itself leaps from one thing to the other, because it forgets itself and thus cannot grasp any definite possibility' (Stambaugh, p. 342).

The world, depleted of its futurity, becomes obscure, is experienced as something unknown and strange; the being-there then begins to update, to make present the most immediate that in its confusion believes should be protected. Heidegger gives the example of fire victims who, in the desperation to escape, save the most irrelevant things simply by them being at hand, immediate. At the urgency of the fear, Dasein forgets him-herself. Thus the temporality of fear is anchored in a form of the past, having-been, the forgetting, which in turn modifies the future and the current (actual) present: 'The temporality of fear is a forgetting that awaits and makes present' (1993, p. 149).

By its turn, in anguish we do not fear for something in particular, for we have nothing that makes sense to fear; we confront ourselves with the emptiness and strangeness of the world into which we were thrown. The world of everyday occupations that is taken as the only reality loses relevance and Dasein can then be vacated, making room for the potentiality of being. The future in anguish cannot be the same as fear, because freed from the occupations Dasein does not await, nor surrender to expectations, because it is before itself. In the same way, the past does not appear as oblivion but as a willingness for the possibility of repetition. As for the present, it is 'held in bringing oneself back to one's ownmost throwness', in revealing the character of possibilities of conjunctures and contexts that, in fear, are frozen and threatened of being lost. While anguish seems to be particularly related to the future as a resolution, fear is anchored in the up-to-dateness (*atualidade*) of an ever-unstable present in its apparent stability.

But it is certainly in the description of the temporality of understanding and falling prey that we can find the most direct contributions to develop our argument. Being an existential, understanding in Heidegger's account cannot be grasped as a category of a theory of knowledge, as in opposition, for example, to explanation. Human existence is understanding, everything it does or does not do is guided by understandings rooted in its condition of being always somewhere, which it can naturalize and accept as an immutable reality, or by understanding its own condition of being without absolute determinations, to questioning itself in its meanings. Heidegger calls disclosedness the condition that allows this questioning, in which the human can then decide on projects that assume past-present-future as a unit. It is the temporality of this articulation, that is, of the disclosedness, that is at the centre of his analysis between paragraphs 67 and 70 of *Being and Time*.

Understanding, deciding and projecting are gestures that are particularly related to futurity. Heidegger attributes an exceptional value to Dasein's ownmost projecting towards itself, as the most definitive dimension of his ontological singularity, and here it is worth remembering that the 'analytic of Dasein', that is, the search for its particular existential structures, is not an end in itself in *Being and Time* but a preparatory path towards the question of the meaning of being in general. Analytics is not meant to be an exhaustive description of the diversity of human existence but of the more original ones. That is why the proper dimension holds a prominent position, even considering that initially and for the most part we are undecided and closed. It is in the disclosure and resolution that we show our most particular condition. Dasein is not only its world but the world's possibility. Thus, proper and improper establish a relationship of mutual dependence, because always fallen in a world that preceded it, it is only from this world that Dasein can be itself.

Understanding is initially and for the most part guided by the improper temporalization of the future. It does not mean that in the improper mode it lacks the future but that this relation is a specific form of the preceding one. The proper mode of precedence is called anticipation. Thus, in the decided disclosedness, the human temporalizes as a project and the future is then given as anticipation. But initially and for the most part he or she is busy, dealing with things inside the world. It is in this occupation, which is a form of understanding, that Dasein continually engages itself in expectations and hopes. What needs to be done? What will I do tomorrow? How will I organize myself to do what is urgent? Thus, in its daily preoccupation with things, Dasein is continually ahead of itself.

Of course this precedence is based on expectations and awaitings. In this inauthentic daily life, Dasein expects that his expectations will be fulfilled, that tomorrow will not be very different from today: on Tuesdays I give classes; next Tuesday I will give classes and I hope that the world and myself can fulfil the expectations of this awaiting. This improper precedence counts with a certain stability of the changes, although it can also wait for the refusal of those expectations and prepare for its frustration. Thus, the improper future of understanding is awaiting (*gewärtigens*).

As for the future of proper understanding, the resolution that founds anticipation is capable of disclosing what Heidegger calls the situation: 'In resoluteness the present [*gegen-wart*] is not only brought back from the dispersion in what is taken care of nearest at hand, but is held in the future [*zukunft*] and having-been [*gewesenheit*]' (1993, p. 135). This form of present articulated by the resoluteness is named as the moment (*augenblick*), in contrast to the now (*jetzt*) of improper temporality. Whereas the now indicates only time as a neutral and homogeneous unit in which we can mark the occurrence of something, the moment is the establishment of a situation, a time that restructures what comes to the encounter in the world. If the form of the future in proper understanding is anticipation, the past appears as repetition. Thus, the situation means assuming that all three temporal ecstases can derive from each other; the past is here and in front of us, just as the future is in the present and in the past. The establishment of a specific temporal situation is precisely a resolution that assumes and reveals the moment as a temporalization of temporality.

The specific form of the present temporalizes in the improper understanding Heidegger calls the making present (*gegenwärtigen*). In a way, the making present is the answer to the experience of time as an empty succession of nows, it is the way in which Dasein intends to keep before itself this succession. The world, then, can only be present because it automatically makes itself present, as if this almost magical maintenance of its presence was of the nature of things. To this making present awaiting (*gegenwärtigendes gewärtigen*) naturally corresponds a past. The foundation of this past, able to maintain Dasein in its daily occupations, is the forgetting of its more proper condition, and so relates to the past data in the oscillation between remembering and forgetting in constant recalling. Memory is a constituent part of the making present awaiting. For Heidegger, this ecstatic unity awaiting-making present-remembering is the basis of the irresoluteness that characterizes the everydayness of Dasein. Irresolute, it watches a world that seems to reproduce itself automatically.

But it is the existential structure of falling prey (*Verfallen*) that finds its priority sense in the present – 'making present' – as well as understanding in the future and attunement in the past. Of the three moods that in Heidegger's *Being and Time* are used to characterize the falling prey, idle chatter, ambiguity and curiosity, only the latter receives a more detailed analysis. Curiosity would be based on the willingness to see and to have seen, without Dasein getting from this encounter with the entity understanding elements. This visualization depends on a meeting in a special type of present, which the Brazilian edition translates as *atualidades* (news): 'This present provides the ecstatic horizon in general within which beings can be bodily *present*' (1993, p. 145).

This form of present as *atualidades* (news) is not devoid of future or past but establishes with them improper relations. Falling prey is the only existential structure of being-there that does not have its proper form; the property of Dasein depends on the suspension of falling prey by resolutedness. Curiosity relates to the future, denying any possibility of awaiting or expectation, since everything that interests one must be at one's fingertips; the future is understood only as a space in which things arise, emerge and can be seen currently. The link between the present and the future becomes opaque and obscure, it is from this very link that Dasein escapes in the not detaining itself of the curiosity, since 'when awaiting is ecstatically modified by a making present that no longer arises, but pursues, this modification is the existential and temporal condition of the possibility of *dispersion*' (1993, p. 146) (Figure 7) "the ekstatic modification of attending [waiting] through the making present that arises in an updating that resurfaces is the temporal and existential condition of the possibility of dispersion [distraction]".

In falling prey, we constantly represent the past as something new (faits divers). The past thus ceases to be in the mode of having-been and presents itself as mere variety in a continuous oscillation between forgetting and remembering. This creates a dispersion that would lead us to perceive the present time as the inability to stay at all, to be everywhere and to be nowhere: 'This mode of the present is the most extreme opposite phenomenon to the *Moment*' (p. 146).

This *atualidade* is seen throughout history, whether of the present or of the future, but it is an identification as a variety of the same, which 'makes present for the sake of the present' (1993, p. 146). The concept of a 'broad present' or 'presentism' shares a clear relationship with the temporality of falling prey, and allows us to comprehend the paradox of a present that is both filled with newness and devoid of events. Regardless of how many new occurrences arise, whether they originate from the past or the future, they fail to reestablish the conjunctural links, since our 'present time' (*atualidade*) predominantly exists or updates itself (almost exclusively) for the sake of the present time alone. What this movement may bring to the presentist argument is to clarify that it is not substantially a broadening of the present but even the broadening of references to the past and future, though in updatist forms. Thus, we can

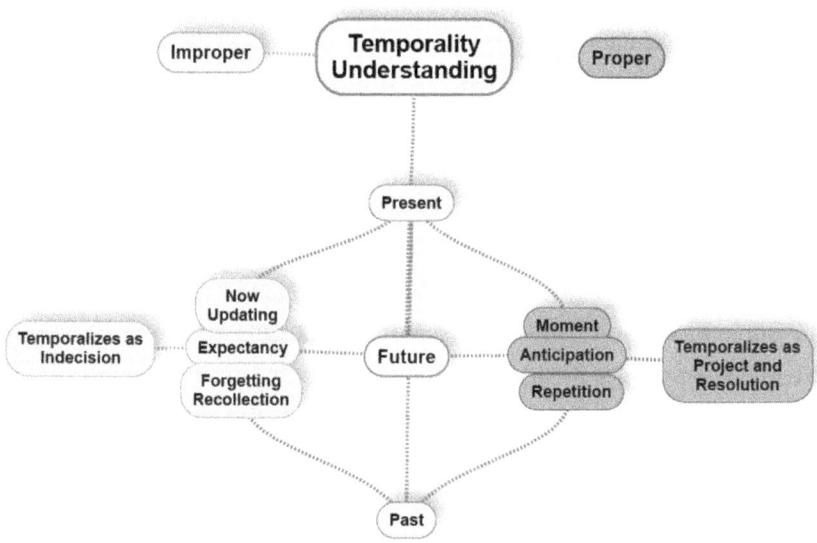

Figure 7 Diagram of the temporality of understanding in Heidegger. *Source*: The authors.

understand how the fascination with history and historical objects can coexist with presentism, or how a society with a closed future can still be addicted to novelty and hungry for the latest TV show, movie, online game or gadget.

It is clear that for Heidegger, Dasein is not devoid of future and past in falling prey, but that the continuous making present (updating) of the current present, what we would like to call 'updatism', prevents Dasein to 'come back to itself' (1993, p. 147). Full of novelties that give the sensation of a rising acceleration, but unable to transform or open the reality for possibilities of difference, in falling prey, there remains to Dasein to always be inside the new, to be up to date with a reality in constant emergence. So the automatic updating that seems to simply pop up on our cell phones and computers becomes a metaphor and an archetypal structure of updatist temporalizations.

As Heidegger is describing ontological-existential structures, they are supposed to be present in any historical horizon. We must then understand falling prey as a transhistorical dimension. What we should think, however, is what factors seem to have broadened the visibility and availability of this temporalization in our contemporaneity. The typically historicist societies of the nineteenth century were also moved for the most part by decadent everyday life, but something prevented this dimension from dominating social self-representation. In the same way, we cannot say that today we have a greater opportunity for distraction, but distraction seems to have become the great social demand. As if life were an endless variety show or a reality show, 'even if one has seen everything, curiosity *invents* new things' (1993, p. 147).

In *Being and Time*, it is the structures of the disposition and the understanding that allow the break with the decadent everyday life. But, as we saw earlier, even these two structures can develop; and in most cases they do so, in an improper way. Also, understanding can temporize more congruently with updatism, despite its structural rooting in the future. In the proper mode, understanding allows Dasein to project itself into its potentiality of being, anticipating the future, repeating the past in what it has of actual, establishing what Heidegger calls the instant (*augenblick*). As for the improper mode of understanding, Dasein relates to the future as an awaiting. The present is the continuous updating of the now, which, obscuring its origin, must always oscillate between forgetting and remembering: 'Awaiting that forgets and makes present is an ecstatic unity in its own right, in accordance with which inauthentic understanding temporalizes itself with regard to its temporality' (1993, p. 136).

Notes

1   For an account of Gumbrecht's intellectual trajectory, see Araujo 2006; Rangel 2010; Rangel and Rodrigues 2012; Brito 2014.

2   On the movement and Lyotard's proximity of the Situationist group, there is a vast literature, within which we highlight Plant 1992.

3   In a similar direction, see Malerba 2014, 2017; Pereira 2015; Araujo 2017; Schmidt and Rodrigues 2017.

4   'These streams are computationally real-time and this is what matters because they provide liveness or nowness for users and contributors' (Berry 2014). The centrality of the streaming concept is best developed by the same author in Berry (2011).

5   This perspective is most evident in the post-1989 period, as Danilo Marques demonstrates in his analysis of 'Postmodern Moralities', published by Lyotard in 1993 (2017, pp. 52–62).

6 On the so-called compensation theories, see Rumiantseva 2015; Mata 2017; Lübbe 2016.

7 It is curious to know that Google's translation tool verifies how to 'update' both the words 'upgrade' and 'update'. The fact that any update today seems to be 'for the better' helps explain this convergence.

8 'The optimistic belief in the future has become obsolete, while nostalgia, for the better or the worse, has never gone out of fashion, remaining strangely contemporary' (Boym 2017, p. 153).

9 Yet, Eduardo Ferraz Felippe, in his dialogue with Gumbrecht, understands current nostalgia 'as a temporal perspective based on an extended present unfolding into a gray future in a time of memory' (2017, p. 124). According to the author, 'the accumulation of the past for those who were born after 1945 [. . .], provides this availability that feeds nostalgia. I dare to say that nostalgic situations carry with them the same symptom of the encounter with the time that Gumbrecht tells us in the works mentioned, a cyclical experience of hope and disappointment' (p. 124). But could not the place of nostalgia today also be understood as a compensatory, reactionary and/or vital necessity of a temporal experience in which a certain current time actualizes/updates itself? Or even the broadening of references to past and future in updatist forms? The author suggests that yes, when he states: 'the motivation provided by nostalgia and the impermanence of the kingdom of men make the future indefinable, and the present is no longer just a transition between other temporal categories, accentuating the mixture between them all' (p. 131).

10 In one of the earliest formulations of the 'broad past', Gumbrecht took up Heidegger, albeit critically: 'If this is a fair description of one of those specific fascinations that, in our present, drive interest in the past, then we can be sure that Heidegger would have interpreted such enthusiasm for speaking to the dead as a symptom of our "falling prey in the world." Turning to the past, making the dead speak to cross the threshold of death inevitably implies moving away from that future in which our own deaths will occur' (Gumbrecht 2003, p. 66).

11 For some recent analyses of Gumbrecht's reflection on modernity, see Brito 2014; Rangel and Rodrigues 2012; Rangel 2010. And also, Araujo 2006, 2013a; Kleinberg and Ghosh 2013.

12 About the movement, see https://en.wikipedia.org/wiki/Gray_Panthers, accessed on 25 September 2018.

13 https://www.oficinadanet.com.br/post/13976-os-riscos-de-nao-atualizar -softwares accessed on 20 September 2018.

14   On the topic, see Ungureanu (2015). The author analyses the relationship between art, self-sacrifice and 'theater of violence' in the episode, understood as a parable of power and resistance in the age of technology. On the habit of watching serial audiovisual narratives through the stream mode on the internet, narrative structures and the compulsive aspect of these practices, see Oliveira (2015a, 2015b). We emphasize that, for this author, 'the mode of reception of audiovisual serial narratives is new, made possible by the Internet and the higher data transmission speed. And it was clearly due to this new modality that interest in serial narratives made a significant leap. The reception of novels and feature films certainly found a place in the new medium, but it was precisely the format of the series that grew unambiguously' (Oliveira 2015b, p. 300). In general, 'the pleasure of the restart is at hand immediately' (2015b, p. 305).

15   Perhaps it is a very unilateral and provincial argument (in the sense of addressing the French and Western European context more directly) to say that the authority of historical discipline over the past has been surpassed. At this point, Malerba (2014, 2017) helps us understand that there are, after the advent of the internet, changes in the history producer and the expansion of the consumer public. The struggle to incorporate the full potential of new technologies, but from the old practices of historical research, led to the questioning of objectives and methods consolidated within the profession, as well as narrative forms. "The rigid division we are familiar with between producers (university-trained men and women on the foundations of history as science, source management and the critical method) and consumers of past knowledge is intended to some extent to safeguarding the autonomy of professional historians. The process of vertiginous expansion of the protagonists and means of circulation of history, however, puts that division in question. [. . .] It would be a mistake, however, to suppose that the impact of Web 2.0 is only by dispersing its productive power. There is also convergence: people are coming together and working to produce a different kind of history. This new online world of public history lacks none of the nuances and dynamism that have characterized the field since its inception. Participation, audience and exposure issues are as complex as they always have been, but the digital platform exponentially enhances them" (2017, pp. 143–4).

16   At this point, of course, our arguments move away from or complexify those of Hartog, as will become clear throughout this book. Insofar as for this author, 'l'histoire, celle du régime moderne d'historicité, avec un grand H ou un petit h, avait foi dans le progrès, marchait au futur et renvoyait avec assurance le passé au passé. Il ne pouvait que passer. C'en est fini, et nous nous sommes retrouvés en tête à tête avec la mémoire et le présent seul' (p. 72).

17 Perhaps this dichotomized perspective in which the French historian thinks
of the relationship between historiography and memory is still very tributary
to Nora's works and the French sociological tradition since Halbwachs. This
permanence is curious despite the criticism of this tradition made, in particular,
by Ricoeur, an important author for Hartog's reflections.

18 Thus, it is probably the incorporation of a phenomenon analysed by Rodrigo
Turin (2017, p. 65), from Hartmund Rosa's reading, in the following terms:
'contemporary acceleration, however, is distinct from that of classical modernity,
since the distance between the horse and the train is smaller than the distance
between the speed of the train and the "real time" of digital information streams.
Moreover, this distance is not only reduced by measuring a higher speed, but
also by its new quality, increasingly devoid of any structuring telos'. In this
sense, Dipesh Chakrabarty (2018, p. 10), in text dedicated to François Hartog,
states: 'Hartog, of course, tells a European – though not Eurocentric – story of
a modern "regime of historicity" (a vision of an open future time) in Europe
that spanned the 18th and 19th centuries and which came to an end with the
two world wars and succumbed to a "presentism" – the future crumbling into
the present – at the end of the twentieth century. It can be argued, however,
that a renewed regime of modern historicity had a second life outside Europe
since the 1950s, when the decolonization of new nations fell under the guise of
modernization theories emanating from the Soviet Union and the United States
during the Cold War era. Incidentally, Ursula Heise describes the anthropocene
precisely in terms that resemble Hartog's description of presentism, "as a future
that has come"'. Does not the argument that peripheries are *not yet* in a certain
experience naturalize the notions of underdevelopment, time, and progress? And
does it not end up assuming a teleological conception that Turin identifies as
being increasingly evanescent and/or nonexistent?

19 In view of some points of our argument, Aurelia Valero and Guillermo Zermeño
make the pertinent comment of a version of this reflection already published
(Pereira and Araujo 2017): 'on the edge of this contrast, the potential error of
regretting or censoring the course that has acquired the temporal experience
of our days is evident, without taking into account the myriad of possibilities it
offers. No less obvious is the need to clarify the assumption of a one-dimensional
and homogeneous temporality, implicit in the presentist argument, and to
recognize the plural nature that characterize it [. . .]. The historian's task would
be, from that perspective, to assume a critical posture, open to chance and
capable of detecting the implications, whether positive or negative, of our new
situation in a time governed by the current' (Valero& Zermeño 2017, p. 9).

20   We follow the translation of Marcia de Sá Cavalcante (Heidegger 1993), comparing it with the Spanish translation by Jorge Eduardo Rivera (Heidegger 2003), the American English translation by Joan Stambaugh (Heidegger 2010) and the original German edition (Heidegger 2006). Calvalcante's work has some peculiarities, such as the translation of Dasein to presence.

21   On the relationship between attunement and temporality, see Lythgoe 2014.

22   For a critical view of Heidegger's reflection on historicity, see Trüper 2014 and Nova 2017. On the political-academic uses of Heidegger's critique of contemporary theoretical-historiographical reflection, see Kleinberg 2007.

2

Updatism and historicism

Chateaubriand and modernity as temporal *mélange*

In his influential essay, François Hartog characterizes the passage from what he calls the ancient regime of historicity, often confused with the *topos historia magistra vitae* and the notion of exemplarity, to a modern regime between the eighteenth and nineteenth centuries from the analysis of three authors: Chateaubriand, Volney and Tocqueville. But it is indeed Chateaubriand that serves as the main guide to this section of the book, being characterized as a man between two worlds or historicities. The idea is a re-appropriation of an excerpt from the *Memoirs* of Chateaubriand himself, who in 1833 interprets his biography as a testimony of the turn of the eighteenth to the nineteenth century, as the meeting between two worlds, the confluence between two rivers, seeing himself as leaving behind the old world to initiate a new and unpredictable course (Hartog 2015, p. 66).

The text that will serve as an emblem for Hartog's description of the passage or succession between the ancient and modern regimes of historicity is in the preface-testament of the *Memoirs from Beyond the Grave*, the often mentioned phrase: *Je me suis rencontré entre les deux siècles comme au confluent de deux fleuves*. A rereading of the *Memoirs* may offer us some interpretative alternatives and perhaps some elements for an different approach of the modernization process and its relations with our enquiry into the concept of updating and the description of updatism.

2.1. Job: Metaphysical certainty and life as a constant updating

Surprisingly, Hartog does not analyse the epigraph chosen by Chateaubriand to open the preface-testament which seems to offer an important reading key for the *Memoirs'* project. It is a very popular Latin interpolation of the book of Job, one of the heroes of the return to Christianity on historicist bases promoted by Chateaubriand's generation. The epigraph appears as follows: *Sicut nubes . . . quasi naves . . . velut umbra* (CHATEAUBRIAND n.d., p. XLIII). These expressions are ways of referring to the speed of time and the fugacity of life, which would pass like a cloud, a boat or a shadow. As we can see below, this is a reference to the central images of different chapters:

> As a cloud dissolves and is gone, so he who goes down to Sheol never ascends again. (Job 7.9)
>
> My days run hurrying by, seeing no happiness in their flight, skimming along like a reed canoe. (Job 9.25-26)
>
> Man, born of woman, has a short life yet has his fill of sorrow. He blossoms, and he withers, like a flower; fleeting as a shadow, transient. (Job 14.1-2)

This ancient reference, in this case Christian, to the lack of sense of the world, which could invite to the *carpe diem*, to the concentration on the present and the pleasures of life, both in Job and in Chateaubriand serves as a pretext for the demonstration of a superior source of sense: God for the first; and the constant reflection on oneself in the case of the *Memoirs*, which must take the beyond-grave point of view to make sense, although recourse to the divine is not foreign to Chateaubriand. This diversity of time receives, in the memorialist effort, a kind of significant fusion. In evoking Job's example, the writer and essayist responds to the tribulations of his time with a renewed bet on the meaning of things, notwithstanding in the key of remembrance: 'I have successively crossed the empty years of my youth, the years so full of the republican era, the splendor of Bonaparte and the realm of legitimacy' (CHATEAUBRIAND n.d., p. XLIV).

The recovery of memories, in a period of life that Chateaubriand wished to have been similar to the stillness he experienced only in the womb and waited again in death, was a kind of paradox that sustained the gesture: how to make sense of a life that was still running and transformed incessantly?

This paradox does not stop the narrative gesture, but invites it. Thus, the life that accelerates must be simultaneously and constantly narrated-updated, but from an anticipatory decision, obviously highlighted in the title *Memoirs from Beyond the Grave*. As we shall see, this solution is not capable of solving all the dilemmas that Chateaubriand believes defy his time. Sufficient for the author, on the social-historical level he would find Job and his faith again.

2.2. The current world: Two impossibilities?

In a passage from the end of *Memoirs* dated from 1841, Chateaubriand states: 'The world today, the world without consecrated authority, seems placed between two impossibilities: the impossibility of the past and the impossibility of the future' (Chateaubriand 1850, p. 6). Between these two impossibilities, there remained the negative gesture of a constant updating of the present. Was it negative because of the finding of the impossibility of alternatives? Was the author of *The Genius of Christianity* frozen in a kind of melancholy-nostalgic presentism? This negative updating would also have its positive developments in the nineteenth century, as the formulation of the Brazilian writer José de Alencar shows: 'The superstition of the future seems to me as dangerous as the superstition of the past. It consists of the true religion of progress in the belief of the present, strengthened by the respect for traditions, developed by aspirations to greater destiny' (Alencar in Lynch 2017, p. 337). Alencar's solution demonstrates how the historicist belief in progress does not always lead to futurism, but to a determination of past and future by the present. Let us avoid this detour, for we are interested in understanding the nature of this updating in Chateaubriand.

In his book, Hartog interprets the double impossibility as the first formulation of the breaking of time that would characterize the entry into the modern regime of historicity (Hartog 2015, p. 88).

However, it is not clear whether first to Chateaubriand or to the French, European or even global context, for certainly before 1841 many other authors had already formulated this situation of breaking the continuity of time, and it is enough to quote Hegel in 1807 in the preface to *Phenomenology of Spirit*. Hartog's citation, in fact a paraphrase of the original, omits the reference to the problem that would produce these impossibilities, the absence of consecrated authority, as well as the rhetorical aspect of the statement, at the end of the text, when Chateaubriand will reveal the key with which these two impossibilities could be overcome: Christianity. Thus, we hope to be able to demonstrate that modernity cannot be reduced to futurism and that presentist or passéist moments are also constitutive of modern temporality. The historicist solution of the reconstruction of narrative continuities, although quite popular, was not the only possibility developed to solve this equation.

It should also be noted that Chateaubriand does not mention the expression 'modern world', but 'current world'. In fact, he uses the word 'modern' less to designate the new world that emerged between the eighteenth and nineteenth centuries, and more to characterize the period of European history since the Renaissance, as in the passage: 'Camoes among the moderns composed the most magnificent epitaphs' (Chateaubriand 1850, p. 246), or when he claims that the medieval French monarchy 'linked the ancient world to the modern' (Chateaubriand 1850, p. 441).

Hartog's reading seems to archaize Chateaubriand, as if only in 1841 (or in 1826 with notes to the *Essay on Revolutions*?) he could be aware of the growing distance between past and future. However, in the conclusions of the *Memoirs* it is very clear that this distance or this crisis was currency for its generation. In a sense, the old world which he witnessed to be undone was the modern world, here opposed to the classical world, but capable of establishing relations of continuity with it, as we shall see below.

2.3. A present without form: The updating of the verb

The concluding chapter of the *Memoirs* is divided into seven parts, a sort of introduction and two well-defined groups, the first devoted to the past and the second to the future. The part dedicated to the past, to the old order that seems to be dragging itself until the present time, ends in the following way: 'The invasion of ideas succeeded the invasion of the barbarians; the current decomposed civilization is lost in itself; the vessel that contains it did not pour the liquor into the other vessel, it is the vessel that has been broken' (Chateaubriand 1850, t. 11, p. 456). Thus the apparent impossibility of the past derives from the dissolution of its form, bequeathing to the present a content that is lost in itself. The image of the inter-worlds seems inadequate, the idea of the decomposition that mixes the original elements is more faithful to the experience of Chateaubriand, who saw his time as a time without continent, without form, or, as he says, the vase of the past is unable to pour its content (civilization), because the present is amorphous. The social form that existed in the past no longer exists, but neither has it been replaced by another one. Thus, they are not two worlds between which one can be or which may have analogous structures. Without form, the present cannot have passed; without past, it cannot have form. But what about the future? Could this present not be self-founding and guided by the horizon of expectation, as we sometimes characterize the gesture of the philosophies of history?

The first subsection dedicated to the future is entitled 'The Future – Difficulty of Understanding It'. It is in the first paragraph that we find the quotation about the two impossibilities. After showing why the old Europe was impossible, Chateaubriand affirms the equal impossibility of the young Europe. He goes on to point out the reasons for this impossibility of the future, indicating, first, the mismatch between material and moral progress. The weakening of national individualities by the tendency, some have pointed out, to the formation of a global community: 'The madness of the moment is to think that from the unity of peoples there will arise a single man, but that would not lead to the loss of "private feelings"' (Chateaubriand 1850, p. 467).

The decomposition of society and the celebration of abstractly equal individuals would produce a moral emptiness, the loss of contact of man with his infinite and intimate possibilities: 'A man does not need to travel to magnify himself, he bears in himself the immensity' (Chateaubriand 1850, p. 469). What would be of this global society, if there were no more French, Portuguese, Germans and the variety of peoples? How could differences in climate and customs express themselves in this abstract society? What language would serve the global communication, a simplified language, or a system in which everyone could understand the different languages? Chateaubriand goes on digressing into a speculative exercise of this global society dreamed up by philosophical utopias and comes to a fascinating conclusion: 'How can we find a place on an earth enlarged by the power of ubiquity and shortened by the small proportions of a desecrated / polluted globe everywhere? There will be nothing left but to ask science for a way to change the planet' (Chateaubriand 1850, p. 470). Being able to be anywhere, the abstract man would also eventually abstract the landscape, in this desacralizing abstraction he would lose the possibility of finding the infinite and the mystery in that which was nearest and most proper to him. This complete objectification of the planet would condemn man to a wandering in search of what was always within his reach: his infinity and freedom.

We realize that all this description is opposed to a man who can find the infinite in himself and in the world around him. Losing this capacity, he becomes a kind of wandering being, so the final image that will only remain for man to leave the planet in search of the infinite that has always been with him. This image will be retrieved by Hannah Arendt in the famous introduction of her book *The Human Condition* and, furthermore, it seems to be a widespread sensation, without the critical elements, in the social discourse between the 1960s and 1970s with the so-called Space Race. Is it just by chance that precisely in this period the concept of updating also spreads?

The second concluding subsection is dedicated to exploring the images of the future. Chateaubriand reviews all the great utopias of his time. For this reason, the title is only an exhaustive list of these experiments: 'Saint-Simonians – Falansterians – Fourierists – Owenists – Socialists – Communists – Unionists – Equalitarians' (Chateaubriand 1850, p. 471). The text is a long argument showing the impossibility and dire consequences of the future of the new utopias: 'Infinity, for example, is our nature; it prevents our intelligence, or even our passions, from dreaming of unlimited benefits, and will reduce man to the life of a snail, transforming him into a machine' (Chateaubriand 1850, pp. 476–7).

The third and last section develops its answer to survive without a visible future, so it is entitled 'The Christian Idea and the Future of the World'. In this section, he argues that it is only from a Christian-evangelical point of view that it would be possible to understand future society and to meet the demands for improvements both of the defenders of the purely republican idea and of the modified monarchy. In the past of the old European order, Chateaubriand sees the decline of the society and the progress of the individual; in the present, marked by the internal contradictions of this social decomposition, only the Christian idea could offer the key to its recomposition: 'Every act of philanthropy we engage in, every system we dream of in the interest of humanity is nothing else than the Christian idea overturned, renamed and often disfigured: it is always the Word made flesh!' (Chateaubriand 1850, p. 485).

Always updating the divine word that became flesh.[1] Therefore, dissatisfied with the nineteenth-century philosophies of history, with its modern utopias, Chateaubriand seems to adopt as a solution a kind of transcendental updating. In this context, the present becomes the expectation of the actualization/updating of an eternal principle. Continuing his image of the vessel, he asserts that if only one seed were left, and if it fell on a little soil, 'it is enough that in the ruins of a vessel this grain will ferment, and a second incarnation of the Catholic spirit will revive the society' (Chateaubriand 1850, p. 486). Christianity would be the force capable of merging divine, moral and political laws, defined as liberty, equality and fraternity, the motto of the French Revolution, which is brought together by the fusion force of Christianity: 'Christianity, stable in its dogmas, is mobile in its lights; its transformation involves universal transformation' (Chateaubriand 1850, pp. 488–9).

Chateaubriand makes a continuous effort, until the last pages of his memoirs, written over three decades, to update himself and his readers about the transformations in his world – this process does not stabilize before a philosophy of history, there is no immanent metanarrative that could curb this acceleration, only the belief in the value of Christianity as a civilizing force, although without the possibility of an anticipated revelation of the moment of its realization: 'When this desired day? When society will recover according to the secret means of the regenerative principle? No one can say; we do not know how to calculate the resistances of the passions' (Chateaubriand 1850, p. 489). As in every update, the author relies on time, counts on time, not in the same way as the philosophies of history, which also had to distrust time to reserve to the historical subject some decisive agency; without this agency progress could always turn into barbarism: 'These calculations, I know, do not combine with the French temperament; in our revolutions we never admit the element of time: that is why we are always astonished by the results that are contrary to our impatience' (Chateaubriand 1850, p. 490). Providence, as the hidden motor of this story, founded hope as the central gesture of Chateaubriand's experience of history, so that even as it was plunged into a formless present, it could swim with hope towards a future that could not be seen on the horizon. The present time of this updating is not of this world, it is the eternal time that incarnates itself in history:

> If heaven has not yet pronounced its last judgment; if a future must be powerful and free, this future is still far, far beyond the visible horizon; only with the help of this Christian hope are we able to reach it, its wings expand as everything seems to betray, hope longer than time and stronger than misfortune. (Chateaubriand 1850, pp. 491–2)

It seems to us, therefore, that the plurality of the temporal experience in Chateaubriand is less the result of a not yet, of a transitory situation, and more of a conscious refusal to the futuristic historical-philosophical solution.

2.4. The temporal fusion in the *Memoirs* and the *mélange*

In the preface-testament Chateaubriand seeks to qualify his voice of authority by pointing out every aspect of life he has experienced, not just the trips he did but the different roles he has taken and the twists of his life. The theme of the man of two worlds is just one attribute of this authoritative and unique voice. As an observer or traveller, Chateaubriand in *Memoirs* is able to write history because he made it: 'I watched the sites, congresses, conclaves, the reconstruction and demolition of the thrones. I made history, I can write it' (CHATEAUBRIAND nd, p. XLV). His discursive authority stems from his privileged position, less as a man between two worlds and more as a testimony in which these worlds are blended in a profound way.[2] This mixture between the old and the new seems to have been a trait of his generation, but when he looked around he realized that there were only a few left to represent this particular time of crisis:

> I have around me only four or five renowned contemporaries. Alfieri, Canova and Monti disappeared; of its bright days, Italy retains only Pindemonte and Manzoni. Pellico spent his beautiful years in Spielberg's dungeons; the talents of Dante's country are condemned to silence, or forced to languish in foreign lands, Lord Byron and Mr. Canning died young; Walter Scott left us; Goethe left us full of glory and years. France has almost nothing of its rich past, which begins another time: I remain to bury my century, like the old priest who, in the sack of Beziers, would have to ring the bell before dying, so the last citizen would have expired. (CHATEAUBRIAND n.d., p. XLV-XLVI)

Although Hartog's use of the passage emphasizes that this old world that was left behind was something close to the classical world, the old regime of historicity, the complete reading of the preface also reveals something simpler perhaps: the lament of a man who already felt as if he was old, to see the world and the generation to which it belonged disappear. The loss he regrets is not only, or above all, of the classical world, but of very close men who were part of what he regarded as his generation, Goethe, Scott, Byron and so on, who left the scene during the widespread perception of a generational change after the revolution of July 1830 (Milner and Pichois 1996, p. 82). By moving the *topos* of man between two worlds, Hartog renews the more canonical interpretation of the tradition of the history of literature that will emphasize Chateaubriand among the exponents of a first romanticism in which neoclassical and modern influences would coexist until they were normalized by the emergence of the new aesthetic in the first great romantic cultural manifestos. But this reading has been challenged by a conception that seeks to demonstrate the porosities between these sensitivities, as Guilherme Gomes writes:

> Unlike those who followed in the footsteps of Winckelmann, Chateaubriand is not nostalgic of a time that has been lost, nor is he willing to propose as imitation model the great art of the times of Phidias. It is not that civilization that moves him, but the sense of time that ruins all civilizations. Chateaubriand thus places himself at the opening of the century that was properly historical. (Júnior 2014, p. 89)

In the last section of the *Memoirs*, in another recapitulation of the main events of his life, the last paragraph is a kind of epitaph:

> In drawing these last words, this November 16th, 1841, my window, which opens westward in the gardens of the Foreign Missions, is open: it is six o'clock in the morning; I perceive that the pale, broad moon descends on the pinnacle of the *Invalides*, revealed by the first golden ray of the East: it seems that the old world is ending, and the new one begins. I see the reflections of a dawn from which I shall not see the sun. All I can do is sit on the edge of my grave; after that I will boldly descend, crucifix in hand, into eternity. (Chateaubriand 1850, p. 504)

Chateaubriand insists on this image of a world that ends and another that begins, but always with the background of a sort of eternal circularity, the same principles are updated, in a repetition that does not contain exemplarity. In the preface-testament, Chateaubriand understands his life as a drama in three acts: in the first, he was a soldier and a traveller; in the second, during the Revolution, he exercised a literary life; and, after the Restoration, politics. In each of these careers he imagined performing specific tasks: the 'discovery of the polar world', 'the restoration of religion from its ruins' and the offer to the people of 'the true representative monarchical system' (Chateaubriand 1850, p. XLVI).

Another trait evoked in order to justify the special value of the *Memoirs* is the fact that he considered himself as the only modern writer in France in which life and work could be perfectly mirrored: 'traveler, soldier, poet, publicist; it was in the bush that I sang the bush, and in the ships that I painted the sea' (Chateaubriand 1850, p. XLVII). For him, this mixture of work and public life had been common in the past, whether among the great Greek and Roman orators or among the poets of the late Middle Ages and the Renaissance: 'the first geniuses of letters and the arts participated in the social movement. What a brave and beautiful life those of Dante, Tasso, Camoes, Ercilla and Cervantes' (Chateaubriand 1850, p. XLVII). In the particular case of France, where, in the past, poets and ancient historians were not divorced from public life, it would have only been from Francis I that the situation would change, 'our writers have become isolated men whose talents may be the expression of the spirit, but not of the facts of their time' (Chateaubriand 1850, p. XLVII). The argument, of romantic taste, tries to affirm that he lived mirroring the events in its literary activity, being able, thus, to document his time, a time of mixture, perhaps of synthesis between worlds:

> If I am destined to live, I would represent in my person, represented in my memories, the principles, ideas, events, catastrophes, the epic of my time, especially that I saw end and begin a world, and that the opposing characteristics of this end and this beginning are mixed in my opinions. (Chateaubriand 1850, pp. XLVII–XLVIII)

Again, it is not just a man between two worlds, but as a mixture, a fusion of opposing characteristics that would be the mark of his time. His response to the crisis will always be this mixture, a mixture only possible by the coming and going movement of reflection, in which birth enters through death and is restored by the ruins, just as he believed he had done with Christianity. From this mix, perhaps a better life could be restored by the old world ruins present at Chateaubriand.

The image cited by Hartog to illustrate the passage between regimes of historicity follows precisely after this clarification and this praise of the mixture. After saying that these two worlds are mixed in him, Chateaubriand writes:

> I found myself between the two centuries as at the confluence of two rivers; I plunged into its turbulent waters, distancing myself reluctantly from the old shore where I was born and swimming with hope to the unknown shore where the new generations will come. (Chateaubriand 1850, p. XLVIII)

He is not between two times, he seems to be aware of being immersed in a formless present (*atualidade*), in which conflicting principles are mixed. In the critical and decisive moment, when the two rivers collide and the waters become turbulent and turbid, he plunges himself, voluntarily or not, into this conflictive environment. Just as the new world that arises from conflict must be a mixture of opposing principles, Chateaubriand also poses himself as a confusion of these worlds: he documents this mixture, it is not only a remnant or the permanence of the old, or the emergence of a new time in all sense different, this confluence will produce a fusion, only in this way one understands how he could 'swim with hope to the unknown shore'. The opening of a new time can only be understood in this mixture of two worlds, hence the privileged position of the *Memoirs* and Chateaubriand not only as one who crosses, but as one who is immersed and involved, an aspect not explored by Hartog, which, in the introduction of his book, highlights only the image of the swimmer who crosses the gap between the old and the modern (Hartog 2015, p. 11).

The figure of a man between two worlds does not seem to reveal all the complexity of this image of a dip, even if it is involuntary, in the turbulent confluence of two rivers. Everything seems to suggest the image of a new epoch as the mixture, not necessarily synthetic, of these principles, the old and the new, irremediably involving contemporaries. The image of the rivers seems closer to the situation of modernity as cascades that precipitate in succession, as described by Gumbrecht (1998). Such an image would avoid the risk of assuming a regime of classical historicity of an unlikely too-long duration or low analytical operability, and would make us pay more attention to the accumulations of these discontinuous processes. It is Chateaubriand himself who offers us, in the *Memoirs*, an accurate picture of this situation:

> Moments of crisis produce a fold in the lives of men. In a society that dissolves and recomposes, the struggle of the two geniuses, the shock of the past and the

future, the mixture of old and new customs forms a transitory combination that does not leave a single moment of boredom. (Book V, p. 293)

It would be very difficult to imagine that in the struggle of geniuses, principles, the past would be completely abandoned, or that the emerging society of this transitory situation would represent only the new, and not another harmony, a provisional one for Chateaubriand, between the conflicting principles in this society which 'dissolves and recomposes'. On the same page, the author offers us a new clue in the same direction, saying that he could better portray French society between 1789 and 1790, comparing it to the architectural elements of the fifteenth and sixteenth centuries piled up by the revolutionaries at the Convent of Petits-Augustin:

When the Greek orders mingled with the Gothic style, or rather, they were assimilated to the collection of nobles and tombs of all centuries, heaped up after the Terror in the Cloisters of the Petits-Augustins: only the wreckage of which I speak is alive and varying without cease. (CHATEAUBRIAND n.d., p. 293)

Figure 8 'Napoleon I and Josephine visiting the Museum of French Monuments with Alexandre Lenoir', Anonymous French, Paris, Louvre Museum, D.A.G. *Source*: : https://en.wikipedia.org/wiki/Alexandre_Lenoir#/media/File:Alexandre_Lenoir_avec _Napol%C3%A9on_et_Jos%C3%A9phine_au_Mus%C3%A9e_des_monuments_fran %C3%A7ais.jpg, accessed on 25 September 2018.

This situation of mixing among the monuments confiscated by the revolutionaries was remedied in 1795 by Alexandre Lenoir, who, since 1791, had been in charge of organizing the estate in order to make it a historical museum. Lenoir then decides to order the collection by reigns and centuries.[3] Here we can have a very concrete idea of the image evoked by Chateaubriand, not of the chaotic heap of Terror, but of the new harmony produced by Lenoir (Figures 8 and 9).

What interests us most in this evocative image of a heap of ruins is the final evocation of Chateaubriand's own position in front of his world: 'the wreckage of which I speak is alive and changing without ceasing'. Far from being the subject of melancholy meditation, or taming in a historicist-museum compensation, the ruins of this world are living principles that can be updated in the present.

Figure 9 The fourteenth-century sculpture room at the Musée des Monuments Français. The French archaeologist Marie Alexandre Lenoir (1761–1839) in the foreground. Painting by Charles Marie Bouton (1781–1853) 1815 Sun. 0.6 × 0.73 m Paris. Carnavalet Museum. *Source*: https://collections.louvre.fr/en/ark:/53355/cl020031508, accessed on 25 September 2018.

2.5. Chateaubriand, our contemporary?

At every moment Chateaubriand uses the metaphor of the boat and the shipwreck to refer to the troubled course of his life which, in the end, does not seem as much a defeat as Hartog analyses, given the awareness of his protagonism: 'Within and alongside my century, I may have unconsciously exercised upon it a threefold influence: religious, political, and literary' (CHATEAUBRIAND n.d., p. XLV). This troubled life seems to surrender itself to the river of history, since the old river merges and mixes with the new one. *Memoirs*, in the back and forth movement, blends the times, challenges the history process in its linearity, almost brushes against the grain, but somehow it already presupposes this unity of modern experience. The image of Chateaubriand as a nostalgic seems more to reflect the position of Hartog himself, and, in a sense, the French civilizational project, in the Western context post-Cold War and post-September 11th.

It seems certain that Chateaubriand saw himself at the confluence between two worlds, two eras, as well as many of his generation since the turn of the eighteenth century. What does not seem evident to us is that these worlds can be well understood as an illustration of distinct temporal regimes; the perception of a passage between worlds is a modern *topos*, and it will certainly be evoked on several other occasions, even when the change in question does not involve temporal transformations of this magnitude. We can think, for example, of Joaquim Nabuco in Brazil, at the time of the Proclamation of the Republic in 1889 (Lynch 2012). Examples are many and times are varied.

Less than the record of this passage between two temporal regimes, memories arise for Chateaubriand as the interpenetration of different times of its biographical trajectory. The essayist states that in joy and bonanza he will write about penury and tribulation; and, in the hours of despair, he will write about his prosperity. Such an attitude would permit another mix, from yesterday to today . . . 'from my cradle to my grave and from the grave to the cradle'.

> The diverse feelings of my various ages, my youth penetrating into my old age, the severity of my years of experience grieving my light years, the ray of my sun, from dawn to sunset, crossing and merging like the scattered reflections of my existence, give a kind of indefinable unity to my work: my cradle has my grave, my grave has my cradle. (CHATEAUBRIAND n.d., p. XLVIII)

After using the metaphor of life as a boat and a shipwreck, he says of the desire to resurrect after the hour of the ghosts to correct the manuscrits of his memories . . . the dead go fast. Reflexivity or second-order observation, or history in and for itself, even with the ontological difficulties that make the gesture if not paradoxical, infinite. The literary activity of Chateaubriand, marked by the constant rewriting, revisions and re-editions reach in their *Memoirs* their apex, in an incessant gesture of updating a report impossible to complete. Again, the idea of repetition and ruin seems to lead less to nostalgia and more to a proper updating, without expectation of resting or accomplishment of a narrative of progress.

At the conclusion of his book, Hartog returns to Chateaubriand to assert him as a non-contemporary. As for the presentism the future would be interdicted, opaque, it would not be possible to repeat this gesture of being between two times. As we saw earlier, this passage from the old to the modern regime is demonstrated by Hartog through the analysis of different moments of Chateaubriand's work; although we have concentrated on the *Memoirs*, the analysis starts from the *An historical, political, and moral essay on the old and modern revolutions considered in its relations with the French Revolution* whose first edition in 1797 is used to demonstrate the old side of the equation, and its second edition, dated from 1826, especially in the new notes added by the author reviewing various aspects of the text, would demonstrate Chateaubriand already inserted in modern historicity.

We believe that, in his reading of the 1797 essay, Hartog allowed himself to be influenced by the notes of the second edition of 1826, producing a sort of retrospective distortion of the first edition. Without denying the substantive presence of aspects of the neoclassical experience in the *Essay* (ER), we believe that it can be interpreted within the philosophical and hypothetical histories so popular in the eighteenth century in Europe and with which Chateaubriand was quite familiar. Therefore, instead of simply interpreting the author as a man between two regimes of historicity, we believe that it would be more productive to understand him as reacting to the modern space of experience from the conceptual and analytical repertoire he had, modern here defined as a moment of loss of the unified form of time. This simultaneity of references was only possible when a modern space of field experience emerged on the historical horizon. Affirming the availability of this field of experience is not the same as saying that all the articulations capable of processing it in ideologies were already available, since, for Koselleck (1999, 2006), ideologization is one of the later phenomena in the history of conceptual modernization.

But, on the other hand, the emergence of modern ideologies will not render unavailable concepts, images and metaphors inherited from other historical moments. Thus, the mere coexistence of these elements seems insufficient to affirm the coexistence of distinct *temporal regimes*, except in the risk of reducing historicity to its simple representation, removing the category of all the socio-political structures that are fundamental in the analysis of the problem in Koselleck, whose research is evoked as a basis for Hartog's argument.

Thus, perhaps we can understand Hartog's somewhat paradoxical statement in his conclusion by saying that our time could no longer be characterized as a time between two worlds as Chateaubriand and Hannah Arendt did, that the dissociation between past and future would have widened so much that we should doubt the very existence of a *historical time*, in the way Koselleck defined it:

> Today, lights are produced by the present and only by it. In this sense (only), there is neither past nor future, nor historical time, if it is true that modern historical time is set in motion by the tension created between the space of experience and the horizon of expectation. (Hartog 2003, p. 218)

Although he seeks to give a restrictive aspect to this characterization, it is noticeable throughout the book that the description of presentism always slips into the idea of a present only time. The problem with this reading is that it considers *historical time* to be synonymous with modernity. Koselleck defines modern historical time not as a tension between experience and expectation, but as the accelerated separation between one and the other; the possibility of distancing crises is embedded in the very characterization of modern time, which Hartog tends to define as something specific to the presentism is a trace of modernity: always mediating and remedying this gap between past and future. Koselleck defines historical time as a transcendental category, presupposes only some kind of mediation, of relation, between horizon and expectation. The lack of historical time would only be possible in a post-human situation. Thus, it seems to us that Hartog fuses modern historical time with historical time in general. Just so that there is no doubt, let us return to these definitions in Koselleck:

Thus our two categories indicate the universal human condition; or, if we so wish, refer to a previous anthropological data. (Koselleck 2006, p. 308)

Historical time is not only a word without content but also a grandeur that modifies itself with history, and whose modification can be deduced from the variable coordination between expectation and experience. (Koselleck 2006, 309)

My thesis states that in the modern age the difference between experience and expectation increases progressively. (Koselleck 2006, 314)

Conceiving of presentism as a sort of post-human temporal anomaly, it is natural that Hartog finds it difficult to find elements of contemporaneity in Chateaubriand. Our reading proposes a displacement of emphasis, emphasizing instead the idea of mixture (*mélange*) as a decisive category to understand the meanings of Chateaubriand's reflection on modernity. In this way, the author of the *Memoirs* can serve as an inspiration in confronting our updatist situation in a way that is not melancholy or nostalgia. In rejecting the philosophies of history and its historicist solutions, it is true that Chateaubriand had in his Christian faith a space of hope that cannot be ours, but beyond this horizon there are other elements which we consider to be more fundamental. It helps us to identify elements of criticism to the effects of modernization that feed our repertoire when we try to characterize presentism, the broad present, or updatism as the forgetfulness of what is most proper to the human, demonstrating that such elements of criticism are not exclusive to our time, something we have already tried to demonstrate in the section on Heidegger.

In a way, our contemporary situation is similar to the Saint-Augustin convent before its musealization; the new digital tools democratized the access to the material vestiges of the past, in order to weaken the synthetic-guiding capacity of the historical discourse. We should not see this situation only for its negative aspects because, besides being irreversible, it would not make sense to expect that this accumulated and available inheritance would be disciplined again. The perception of the loss of the form of time in Chateaubriand seems to be potent in guiding our current experience.

Finally, Chateaubriand also teaches us to identify, in this multiplicity, living ruins of the past that can be evoked and updated to meet the plural demands of our plural time. Betting and accepting fragmentation and temporal mixing as a more liberating possibility than just historicist synchronization, even knowing that it is still a possibility among others, but cannot be taken as a synonym of historical time. Betting on the ability to make the fragment in ruin alive as a strategy to meet our existential, practical and cognitive demands in our relationship with history.

Hartog's description of presentism as a disoriented time also does not match our description of updatism as a time when people also seem to rely on an automatic organization of reality. Thus, our situation does not simply emerge from a disoriented time, without telos, but from a society in which people feel that they need not to have to worry about this kind of orientation, that the updating of the present would be guaranteed in some way, or out of reach of their agencies. Certainly there are dangers that need to be avoided in this situation. We can learn a lot by reactivating the synthetic and guiding capacity of historical discourse, but without waiting or hoping for a restoration of the modern situation – perhaps more imagined than lived – of a world full of meaning. Dismissing subjectivities, bodies and minds from this task can release social energy to meet new challenges.

Notes

1 Although the word 'updating' seems to have no relevance or even to have existed in this form in the nineteenth century, the concept is available. In analysing Varnhagen's *História Geral do Brasil*, Themistocles Cezar writes: 'the updating corresponds to the establishment of a proper time for Brazilian history' (Cezar 2018, p. 188).

2 Themistocles Cezar emphasizes the (un)ordered appearance of this time in Chateaubriand (Cezar 2010, pp. 30–31).

3 Françoise Choay (2006) writes of this episode: 'But, first of all concerned with civic pedagogy and the historical education of citizens, he arranged his fragments according to a chronology that seemed to him to be credible'. In addition, 'he was careful, whenever possible, to gather [. . .] everything that could give an idea of the ancient clothing, both civilian, men's and women's, and military, according to patents. The pieces thus assembled should only be seen as a cluster of models, dressed according to the times to which they belong' (p. 103).

Updatist fragments

3.1. Past futures: 2001 in 1970

In the introduction to this book, we present some elements for an initial periodization of the phenomenon of updatism. Whether it is the database of Google Ngram or the Digital Newspaper of the National Library at Rio de Janeiro (BN-RJ), the period between the 1960s and 1970s stands out as the moment of acceleration in the use of the word. A quick foray into some sections of this period of about half a century might be useful. In retrospect, what in the lifeworlds of the year 1970 could indicate the transformation we are describing?

What should or could be updated in the year 1970? It is worth mentioning that in our research in the database of the *Jornal do Brasil* (JB), which in the newspaper archive begins in the 1890s, there is no reference to the words 'to update' or 'updating' until 1922. In 1926, one *'actualisar'* appears with the sense of realization of a potential energy, in a matter about doping in horses. It is only in the 1930s that we see a broader use, much applied to the process of constitutional reform. This weak presence of a verb that seems to us so natural and widespread today should alert us to some discontinuities still barely perceived in the modern experience of time.

As we shall see, in 1970 the word appeared to be relevant at various levels of social life, with widespread use. The choice of just one year, of just one newspaper, is in part due to the effort to put as much of the body of the archive as we can construct in front of the reader in order to tell our history, not because we want to make it just more authoritative by the sources but, as already said, to broaden opportunities for other histories.

After reading all passages in which the word 'update' (*atualizar*) and its lexical variations were used in the pages of *Jornal do Brasil* in 1970, the first conclusion is that the word 'update' was an efficient filter to recover relevant traits of the lifeworlds. In the most diverse sectors, reality could or should be updated: in individual psychology, in work methods, in carnival, in learning in all age groups, in the administration of private and public companies, in their 'control systems, information and decision-making', in general production infrastructure, in the fashion wardrobe of the season or in clothing with some new hardware. Opera, films, literature are also subject to updating. Not only equipment like the computers themselves, which already figure as the great heroes (or villains?) of this process, but also the aircraft, clothes, legislation and politicians should be up to date. It was also necessary to update the land structure and censorship, personal income, the Church, whether in its dogmas or management processes, and the workforce in general. Women, in particular, seemed to be in need of special help to enter this new time. The subject-object of the updating is knowledge and information. We could update ourselves with one's thoughts and dispositions or actualize with 'the latent energies in being' or our astral energies. Update yourself to keep pace with the changes as well as the way you act. Finally, we could update ourselves on something by following the news.

Out of this great diversity of uses we may be able to produce some more general devices to help us understand what we are doing when we update. The first realization is that this universe can be divided between things that update and things that need to be updated, even if sometimes these borders intersect, as in the example of the computer, which appears as the greatest tool to 'update', but it will also be updated at all times, until, perhaps, the updating becomes automatic. We can perceive the feeling that this interval between the current (*atual*) and the out of date (*inatual*) needed to be shortened to the point where there is no distance between these states anymore, that is, a reality with zero index of noncurrentness (*inatualidade*). Perhaps this is a possible formulation of a certain aspect of an updatist utopia or illusion.

Another aspect is the existence of two great semantic fields in the word, to actualize how to effect something that is latent, like the fulfilment of a potential, and to update in the sense of to correspond to the current, the most modern and developed. The first sense seems to be the oldest, we have seen its appearance, albeit with an archaizing spelling (actualizar), in 1926 in the *Jornal do Brasil* series, with the sense of effecting a potential energy, in a matter about doping in horses. The second use tends to become stronger, which may partly explain the normalization of spelling in atualizar, almost eliminating the difference between the *actual* (actual, real) and the *atual* (now, present, current, contemporary, modern). This fusion opens a wide space to the overlapping of the two senses, with a considerable predominance of the second.

We can say that updatism depends on this fusion, so that the real, the effective, is confused with the most current, the most recent. Thus, from the individual point of view, whether in gymnastics (yoga), psychotherapy, behaviour, learning or fashion, fulfilling all its potential means being aware, having access to all information, betting on processes that make ourselves and others available as quickly as possible, on edge, immediately.

The occurrences around the new method of the Programmed Instruction clearly show this set of problems; it promised speed and equal access to the values that would allow every individual to update her or his knowledge about any matter. The immediate aspect of the answers is programmed-modular content – the student needs to reach a minimum number of correct answers to go forward and the answers are available at the end of the exercises – they suggest that the 'programmed' here establishes bridges between education systems and computational systems. Would it be possible to program people as if they were programming computers?

The ambivalent transition between humans and machines is quite old, but it seems to have a special relevance at this juncture. Since 1968 the film *2001: A Space Odyssey* has been playing in Brazil. On 19 June of that year, in a full page in the *Jornal do Brasil*, Miriam Alencar summarized the centre of the plot:

> the astronauts Bowman and Poole travel taking with them three scientists who are kept in sarcophagi with an animated suspension [sic], that is, hibernate, to resuscitate on the spot and the computer Hal 9000, who knows everything, sees everything, speaks everything and everything controls. (JB 06/19/1970)

One of the icons of our time, Stanley Kubrick's and Arthur C. Clarke's film-book condenses and diffuses this sense of a probably lost competition between men and computers. The image of the film evoked by the journalist is terrifying, human beings completely deprived of currentness, in suspended animation (sealed in sarcophagi), exposed to the desires of a computer that knows everything. In Fluxo's propaganda, the allusion to conflict-desire could not be clearer: the text starts with the assertion that computers cannot create, cry or love (and hate?), that their young and super-updated young group of employees could make the connection between you (who knows your business) and the computer. But, as we see in *2001*, the mediators are not always able to mediate, perhaps because they cannot afford to live an 'outdateing' hibernation. In the end, the ad has an almost threatening tone: 'For now, computers do not have self-determination. They do not even have to earn a living.' You, the business owner, who needs to earn a living, cannot stay in suspended animation. Like a *pharmakon*, computers can be the remedy or the poison, as long as they do not become very determined or passionate. The remedy can still be a simple cosmetic, as we will see later.

This theme, which involves opposition, collaboration and even (con)fusion between the human and the computer, develops in parallel with the obsession with the most recent information, such as that of Minister Passarinho, who, in a way that seems naïve today, asks his advisors to make newspapers clippings so that he can be updated with the problem of drug use and trafficking (JB 11/31/1970); or in the case of companies and government agencies that saw in the continuous updating of data processing centres a kind of inescapable action in the struggle for survival (JB 03/24/1970). The complaint about the excess data, which would be common afterwards, does not appear in the JB 1970 series; the central concern is about organization, availability and new forms of data entry, such as brand-new keyboards that promised to replace punch cards (JB 10/16/1970).

The confusion between man and computer demands to be inside, sometimes literally, as the astronaut Bowman was inside Hal9000 to deactivate its memories, deposited in a sealed room, metaphor of the machine brain: 'If it were possible to say that the computer's personality occupied some place in space, it lay in the sealed room, containing the labyrinth of interconnected memory units and processing grids near the central axis of the carousel' (Clarke 2013, Loc.1844).

The so-called reality televison competitions dialogues with this tradition of images, an eye that sees everything, human beings disposed-closed in stations in which the sensations of total confinement, availability and transparency are confused, even if only to hide the real distance that separates the viewer of the show and its (in)transparencies. The question returns, who is inside whom? Is reality a show, or is the show reality? Are we inside the computer, or is the computer inside us? Or there would be nothing else that could be called real, just the virtual. As we discussed, in updatism the real is confused with the current in constant representation. The updatist world is not only the best world possible, it is the only possible world. Frequent updates may not allow for the emergence of truly novel ideas or approaches that break away from the established pattern, resulting in a lack of space for the new in the sense of discontinuity. From an updatist perspective, the new is a catastrophic failure in the system.

The image of being sealed inside something appears several times in the *2001* book as a protective image, either in the capsules that isolate against the rigours of space, or in the hibernation cocoons; but also as prison and death:

> Now the times had changed, and the wisdom inherited from the past had become foolish. The ape-men had to adapt themselves or die – like the larger beasts that disappeared before them, and whose bones now lay sealed within the limestone hills. (Clarke 2013, Loc. 269)

Like the fossils of extinct dinosaurs sealed within limestone hills or in the same cocoons, now imagined as sarcophagi when Bowman needs to empty them of the bodies of the crewmen killed by Hal9000. This parallelism between men and dinosaurs is organized by the image of the necessary evolution and adaptation drawn in the first updating of the hominids at the beginning of the book; also the *Homo sapiens* became obsolete.

The three assassinated crewmembers would be analogous to the extinct dinosaurs or primitive individuals discarded by the computer-obelisk in its quest for the best specimens to be programmed. Bowman would have been the only one selected to receive the new updating. In Clarke's mythology this updating is not produced in its own right, the computer-obelisk coming from space penetrates the mind and body of this ape-man to reprogram it and make it evolve in another direction. Without this interference he would surely be extinguished. The sense of evolution is the struggle against obsolescence that could only be driven by external program forces. The survival of the fittest becomes the survival of the most up to date. Although we are tempted to repeat Tocqueville's celebrated phrase, for here too without the wisdom of the past man would wander in the shadows, there is in the midst of darkness a light, but this light does not seem to belong to human history.

However, by 1970, machines were not just external tools but could also permeate our inner world through programmed instruction, advanced brainwashing techniques that existed in both reality and the imagination, and even in the image of being 'up-to-date' in one's thoughts and disposition (JB 09/24/1970).

In his work, Clarke connected the communication revolution enabled by satellites to potential risks of political manipulation, such as propaganda and brainwashing. He also expressed concern that these risks could stem from a deeper source: a tendency towards banality inherent in human nature.

In JB of 5 February 1970 there is a brief note reviewing the book *Profiles of the Future: An Inquiry into the Limits of the Possible*, a collection of texts by Clarke originally published in 1962. The volume is published in Brazil in the collection 'Presence of the Future', coordinated by Rose-Marie Muraro, a pioneer of the feminist movement, who in the same year published his book *Sexual Liberation of Women*. In the essay 'Voices from the Sky', Clarke develops the theme of the expansion of TV and radio signals and the political uses that the Soviets could make of this new reality:

> This freedom of communication will have an overwhelming effect on the cultural, political and moral climate of our planet. It contains both dangers and promises. If you doubt this, consider the following unimaginative extrapolation, which may be titled 'How to conquer the world without anyone noticing.' Around 1970 the USSR established the first high-power satellite TV above Asia, transmitting in several languages so that more than one billion human beings can understand the programs. (Clarke 1962, p. 397)

The same idea is developed in 1960s 'I Remember Babylon', the first tale of the 1962 *Tales of Ten Worlds* compilation, which recounts an alleged meeting of Clarke with a North American deserter who planned, in collusion with the Soviets, to launch a TV satellite to broadcast all sorts of undesirable content on US territory: 'For the first time in history, any form of censorship becomes totally impossible. There is simply no way to apply it; the customer can get whatever they want in their own home. Lock the door, turn on the TV – friends and family will never know' (Clarke 2000). The libertarian producer wanted to offer content that was censored, such as pornography, for all 'four sexes' [*sic*] and images of torture like the ones revealed by the Nuremberg trials: 'History is on our side. We will use the American decadence itself' (Clarke 2000).

The issue returns in the single passage from the *2001* book, in which any variation of the word 'update' is used.[1] In the journey between the space station and the Moon, Dr Heywood Floyd checks the news on his newspad and reflects on the wonders of communication:

> The text was updated automatically every hour; even if someone read only English versions, it was possible to spend a lifetime doing nothing but absorb the ever-changing flow of information from news satellites. (Clarke 2013, Loc. 709)

The enchantment with technology would soon give way to a severe judgement on its effects: 'The more marvelous the media, the more trivial, mediocre, or depressing its content seemed to be' (Clarke 2013, Loc. 709). There follows a list of ills described in the newspapers – accidents, crimes, conflicts, dark editorials – but all this seemed even better than 'Utopia' newspapers, which, 'he had concluded long ago, would be terribly annoying' (Clarke 2013, Loc. 709).

The impact of the *2001* film/book on the collective imagination of 1970 cannot be overstated. The vocabulary, themes and imagery seemed to feed off each other, blurring the lines between the accelerating sensation of technological progress and the more modest achievements that were actually happening, as well as their impacts on daily life.

During the 1970s, the average person had little to no contact with real computers, but the perceived threat and promise of this new technology was palpable. The imagery and references associated with this emerging field of technology seemed to align perfectly with prevailing ideologies of progress and modernization. The interpretation given to the song '2001' by Rita Lee and Tom Zé at the 1968 International Song Festival, which was introduced by an old Brazilian country music style that indicates that even at the time, contemporaries recognized the ambivalences inherent in this emerging technology:

> I can almost touch it, my life screams
> Impregnates and reproduces at the speed of light
> The color of the sky composes me, the blue sea dissolves me
> The equation proposes me, computer solves me
> Rita Lee and Tom Zé, '2001', 1968[2]

One year later, in another song from the same composer, the imagery of *2001* reemerges, stressing an optimistic/ironic fusion of human and machine:

> It may seem strange to you, the new movement
> Your eyes may be made of copper, your arms of tin
> Don't worry, my system will maintain
> The consciousness of being
> You will think
> Your body will be brighter
> Your mind, smarter
> Everything in super-dimension
> The mutant is happier
> Happy because
> In the new mutation
> Happiness is made of metal.
> Gilberto Gil, 'Futurível', 1969[3]

3.2. Transparency, censorship and repression

The reference that starts our series, dated from 14 January 1970, describes a psychotherapy session that would have taken place in the United States under the supervision of the therapist Paul Bindrim.[4] It was a dynamic group based on the idea that nudity could *accelerate* the healing process; this meant dismantling the social masks and freeing the individual for more transparent and free interactions. The fatigue induced by the very long sections of collective nudity should aid in the dropping of masks, updating 'the potential of normal individuals'. Updating is being used in the sense of realizing a potential, but clearly it is associated with the pressure to be 'inside', to break with entrenched social prejudices, whether it is the masks of repression or conventional morality, a theme that divides societies and generations between the 1960s and 1970s, especially from 1968. After all, being free seems to go through a full display. Closed in themselves, represented by elaborate social masks, these people were invited to live a new transparency. But would not there also be the risk of censorship or false-minded programming?[5]

Three days later, on 17 January, the theme of censorship and repression became less abstract. On the front page of the paper, we see two calls side by side, the first informs that the 'New IBM factory goes to São Paulo', the second, 'Church calls subversion to unity and peace.' The death of soldier Elias Santos in an action against the so-called 'subversion' has become one of the places of memory for those who cultivate the legacy of the Dictatorship. The soldier was killed at the end of December 1969, which explains the somewhat abrupt connection in the article between the archbishop's lament and the news on the creation of what would be one of the most cruel (and updated) apparatuses of political repression, CODI (Operation Center for Domestic Defense). Throughout the year, political repression continued to grow, showing that the 'Center and Internal Defense Operations' that was inaugurated then, with the promise of 'updating' the 'working methods together', would not fail to have its effects. For those who were struggling against repression and censorship, freedom as transparency could only be a dangerous fantasy. For the organs of repression, having greater control, organization and speed in information retrieval justified the use of new transparency control technologies. Of course, controlling transparency and opacity are different things. Governments needed to govern what should be displayed and what could be hidden. Transparency policies, despite some total enunciations, are always a balance between what one should or can show and/or conceal. The promise of full transparency is also a threat.

The intensification of the repression implied the updating of its tools, in addition to the creation of the CODI, and on 18 September we have the news that the Censorship Service had just 'updated the censorship legislation'. The tone of the note is almost celebratory; after all, the federal censor now had a document capable of guiding him in a work that seemed increasingly complex and urgent. It was promised that the TV shows would be examined by three censors and the results drawn in 48 hours. But the task of control also needed to be socially distributed, so the rules that were given to the broadcasts' directors would also serve as a guide for the filmmakers, theatologists and artists, allowing them to self-censure in advance. Even in the sealed room of conscience, censorship was invited in, and no expression seemed to be banal to the point of lack of care, especially to those who exhibited sexual intercourse, vices and immorality. When not forbidden to exhibit, its appearance should be in morally regulated contexts. Of course in the reality of a divided society these orientations would produce very different effects; here we would only like to highlight the desire for control and updating.

3.3. The fear of obsolescence and the superhuman

Much has already been said about the man-computer competition atmosphere that seemed to permeate certain aspects of everyday life in 1970 through the pages of JB. On the one hand, computer skills, projected or imagined, created a feeling that the man would have a new competitor to fear; on the other hand, these same abilities arose as a promise of an expansion of human senses and capabilities. *At the risk of becoming obsolete, the upgraded man could become a superman.* The theme could have a parallel development in which the man had its authenticity reinforced, so as to differentiate it from this new machine that seemed to advance in one of the hitherto exclusive abilities: thought.

All these perceptions were aggravated by the sense of acceleration, whether actually existing or envisioned. Everyone seemed to run the risk of becoming obsolete, of being left out. Thus, in the already mentioned article of programmed learning, the columnist talked with the fears and desires of the readers: the method would teach any subject in less than three months, the active response, the instantaneous application and the immediate evaluation would guarantee the speed. Macroeconomics, chess, medical nomenclature, everything could be quickly learned: 'after all, it's not the first time you feel the need to learn new things, to stop being outside, to update yourself' (JB 03/05/1970). So much information available, not one of them seemed banal for the announcement called 'Programmed Instruction', it was necessary to accelerate the learning, because if everything abounds, the time always lacks: 'To attend a course nocturnal? But you get exhausted from work and the schedule of the course is right up there.' (JB 03/05/1970) Analogous to dynamic reading, programmed instruction was supose to give to humans the processing skills analogous of a computer. Next comes the example of research done among IBM employees, the forerunner of great myths of our time such as Microsoft, Apple and Google – the mother of Hal9000. There is a constant confusion between the universe of cybernetics and education. The goal? 'To go further, by developing the senses of man leading him to see more, to understand better, to feel more' (JB 03/05/1970). As in the ironic formulation of 'Futurível', do not worry, the system will ensure that 'your body will be brighter / Your mind, smarter / Everything in super-dimension'; or the ironic news of 28 August that UFMG – Federal University of Minas Gerais – would have become the first university in Brazil to abolish the entrance exam for people interested 'in complementing or updating their knowledge'.

Body and appearance were particularly sensitive to the risk of outdatedness. It is curious to note, if we only consider the article of 13 October, that gymnastics and bodybuilding were practically nonexistent in Rio de Janeiro in 1970, since the columnist needs to introduce basic concepts, besides pointing out the absence of practice. The 'restful fatigue of gymnastics' seems to have some kinship with the liberating exhaustion of sessions of bare psychotherapy, as well as the actualization of the 'latent energies in being' of yoga, with the updating of the 'potential of normal individuals'. Keeping the current body can mean exploring the cosmetic potential of our *pharmakomputer*, which today is evident from Photoshop to the automatic digital filters of cell phones that keep us younger and updated. This is very consistent with the analysis of 16 and 17 August, which affirmed the country's immense backwardness, its need to 'burn stages of production techniques', which would go through the effort to 'upgrade the workforce'.

In addition, the body also had to fight against the obsolescence of fashion. The invitation from Sears to upgrade the wardrobe to the spring season is just the most familiar aspect of the phenomenon (JB 09/21/1970). The obsession for the future encourages the cultivation of clothes and objects that fantasized a present not yet established but already lived. The accelerated updating of equipment and infrastructure seems to have to match the body and the clothing, in a kind of alignment between hardware and software, which is what, in our series, the note of 28 October on the new uniform of the commissioners of VASP (São Paulo Airways) seems to indicate. The caption of the photo, in which a commissioner appears standing in front of a plane, says: 'The idea of updating the uniform occurs in parallel with the renovation of the equipment used by the company'. The moss-green set, one of the 1970s fashion colours, should look very current. Updating a central element of the context causes a wave of obsolescence that needs to be answered.

Doubts as to the currentness of the human arise again in the 25 November article on the preparations for the launch of the North American space station Skylab.[6] In the early 1970s, the Space Race seemed to have slowed, funding problems and emergencies of other social agendas having deprived some of its centrality. The book *Mars and the Mind of Man* transcribed the debate that occurred in October 1971, on the eve of the arrival of the Mariner 9 spacecraft on Mars (Clarke et al., 1974). The event was part of a large-scale propaganda campaign and included a journalist, Bruce C. Murray, writers and public figures such as Ray Bradbury, Arthur Clarke, Carl Sagan and Walter Sullivan. Murray, in his final remarks, written in a later evaluation for the publication of the debates in 1973, characterized the sense of mismatch between the advances of space science and societies: 'Can the obsolescence of our governmental and social institutions lead us to a constructive evolution with the speed necessary to capitalize on the fantastic scientific foundations recently launched with the Mariner and Apollo explorers?' (Clarke et al., 1973, p. 69). He went on to point out that he was concerned with the obsolescence rate of various institutions such as 'universities, primary and secondary schools, churches, businesses, legislative bodies, professional societies, the National Academy of Science and many others'. In fact, it would be the members of these institutions that 'hardly have time to change their attitude', hence the symptoms, 'a great amount of suicides, insanity and neuroses' (Clarke et al., 1973, p. 101).

There was much discussion about the role that humans could still play in the conquest of space, since the tendency seemed to be the predominance of unmanned missions, at least by people of flesh and blood. Thus, it is understood that the Skylab article states that with the station NASA 'hopes to prove, first and foremost, man's need in the execution of the space program'. The Skylab project stood out precisely by the decision to man a satellite, transforming it into a laboratory with people, since the satellite would not know how to set priorities. The human factor would save the task of information processing: 'Almost every task can be performed by automata, that is true, but in many cases economy and effectiveness can only result from an immediate human decision.'

3.4. A panther's leap into the current

The 22 March event is a review-interview on the movie *Benito Cereno*, filmed by French director Serge Roullet in 1969, in which Rui Guerra plays the title character. The story, based on a tale by Herman Melville, takes place in 1799 and depicts the revolt on a Spanish slave ship. The selected excerpts are speeches by the director, who eventually highlights the temporal intersections that would make his work updated, based on a text written in the nineteenth century, about an incident in the eighteenth century, whose currentness was ironically highlighted by excerpts from one of the leaders of the Black Panther Party, Stokely Carmichael[7] (1941–1998): '*Slavery is not over, the black problem of the eighteenth century is still alive in 1970*' (emphasis added).

As the director refused to use professional actors in his films, he had to look for people who could embody his characters. Finding the types of black Africans that could represent this past lurking in the present was naturally a temporal difficulty. The updated blacks were like the Black Panthers, but even though they were analogous to the eighteenth-century rioters, something separated them, especially from the black ones that one might find in an urbanized area like Rio de Janeiro, contemporaneous but not updated? It was only from the quilombola community of Marambaia that these updated blacks could be found – a kind of temporal island or time capsule.

The quilombola community of Marambaia came with the collapse of the empire of one of the largest slave traders and owners in the Brazilian monarchy, based in the city of Piraí which had an illegal entry point for Africans in the Marambaia coast.[8] In the quilombo the director says he discovered a kind of fossil that, unlike Clarke's hominides, could still have a future: the resolution of a trauma, a temporal knot or an open scar in time: 'The most remarkable thing is that these creatures have been able to preserve their freedom over the centuries'. In this case, the updating presupposes a kind of denunciation of the present, which was still haunted by an ambivalent past: slavery and its effects, but also a legacy of freedom that had accumulated and could move in the present opening new potentialities. Are we here facing an updating in the proper sense? Was this the same effect Autran Dourado had expected from good literature, 'to update, to make language alive', or is it more about the ability to incorporate the present into an already accumulated heritage?

In the JB sports section, Ubirajara da Silva Alcântara,[9] at the time Flamengo's goalkeeper, recounted his disagreements with the controversial former goalkeeper and coach Yustrich (Dorival Knipel, 1917–90).[10] In his words, 'I sometimes think that Yustrich should update their way of acting on and off the field.' The coach, already well known for other controversies, had a reputation of being rigid, this time he had scolded the player for 'appearing in the club with colored pants'. He also complained about Ubirajara's habit of holding the ball too long with his feet during the games. For the young rising star – who in August of that year had scored an unprecedented goalkeeper goal and the following year would be elected in the Chacrinha TV Show 'the most beautiful black man in Brazil' – this generational-sporting conflict could be resolved by an updating of behaviour. In fact, Ubirajara's look denounced the incredible temporal distance, far greater than any calendar could register, that kept him from Knipel. In the early 1970s, when the Black Panther movement reached its peak in the United States, the young man was one of the myth's local updates, not only fashionable but incarnating. His updateness, as a double, made Knipel obsolete, as if there could be no room at that time for the old and current goalkeepers. For Knipel, as for much of that society, this new one was perhaps just another fad, one that could be controlled by the updating of censorship, repression and instruction.

Most of the time the upgrade effort seems to be directed not at reactivating some potential of the past, but in the struggle for survival in ways that were rapidly becoming obsolete. In the occurrence of 12 February, this aspect is quite evident in the demolishing review of the parade of the Great Societies of Carnival. The article points out that the municipal secretary Levi Neves had been asked if it would not be the case to end this kind of parade once and for all, to which he replies: 'you cannot end this way with a tradition of more than 100 years'. The solution: 'is to find a way to update and streamline the parade'. But the efforts do not always succeed, in this case, the Great Societies effectively disappeared from the Brazilian carnival. At the entry of 27 August it is the opera that is in question, and the updating solution also had to be dynamized: just one act, economy in production, scenario with light gears, all in order to make old Rossini more accessible, 'to update the opera itself and revive public interest in the show'.

All these manifestations from the past needed to better represent the current times, the same perception John XXIII had in using the Italian word *aggionarmento* to define the task of transforming the Church. In one of the main documents of the Second Vatican Council, published in 1965, the 'Pastoral Constitution *Gaudium et Spes*' has the subtitle 'On the Church in the Modern World'. Although the derived forms '*actualizar*' (to update) or '*actualização*' (updating) do not appear in any moment, the word '*actual*' (current/up to date) – spelled in Portugal's Portuguese on the Vatican site – appears forty-two times in the document. But this did not prevent the Council's effort to understand the present world from being widely interpreted as 'an effort of the Roman Catholic Church to update itself' or, as in the original English on

3 July, an 'update of the Church'. This better representation of current times implied bureaucratic modernization – with computers and other electronics, but also global representation, reducing the weight of Italians in the Curia.

*   *   *

For the volume, relevance and representativeness, the words 'to update' and 'updating' seem to carry, in the JB 1970 series, the value of a historical-social concept. They point to a new dimension of the experience of time, which develops certain potentialities of modern time, but also points to some of its limits. The pressure to be up to date takes on the contours of an ideology, as it seems to make sense of a joint view of reality. We have also seen that beyond this ideological dimension, in the most basic sense of its ability to aggregate values and make sense of many layers of reality, what we are calling updatism, the concept of updating also holds critical potential when it disrupts the current from the present, when it claims forces from the past (and the future) as more updated than the present ones.

Notes

1 In the Brazilian edition there is a second occurrence, but translating the original 'while he was briefing himself' to '*enquanto se atualizava*', or 'while he was getting up-to-date'.

2 Listen at https://www.youtube.com/watch?v=2BKGMjYCPhc, accessed on 25 September 2018.

3 https://www.youtube.com/watch?v=sAyGHbFx0V0, accessed on 23 March 2023.

4 Cf. https://en.wikipedia.org/wiki/Nude_psychotherapy, accessed on 25 September 2018.

5 Twenty years later, Baudrillard (1996) stated in a melancholy tone: 'If it were to characterize the current state of affairs, I would say that it is that of the post-orgy. The orgy is the explosive moment of modernity, that of liberation in all domains. [. . .] Today everything is released, the game is done and we are collectively faced with the crucial question: WHAT TO DO AFTER THE ORGY? [. . .] Basically, the revolution has happened everywhere, but not as expected. Everywhere what was released was to go into pure circulation, into orbit. With some retreat, it can be said that the inevitable end of all liberation is to foment and nurture networks. [. . .] The logic of the viral dispersion of networks is no longer that of value or

equivalence. There is no longer revolution, but circumvolution, an involution of value [. . .] Thus, the idea of progress has disappeared, but progress continues. The idea of wealth that sustains production has disappeared, but production remains firm [. . .] Today's technological beings, machines, clones, prostheses, all tend towards this kind of reproduction and slowly induce the same process in the so-called human and sexual beings [. . .] At the time of sexual liberation, the watchword was "maximum sexuality with minimum reproduction".

6   For an overview of the project, see Compton (1983).

7   See https://www.google.com/url?q=https://kilombagem.net.br/educacao/ biblioteca/stokely--carmichael-1941-1998-de-pantera-negra-a-pan-africanista/ &ust=1565964660000000&usg=AFQjCNEnh1pexkjH73mNBHVJIivKPL5hDQ &hl=pt-BR&source=gmail

8   In 2015, the community took ownership of the area after a long dispute with the Brazilian Navy. See the news on the website of Incra: http://www.incra.gov .br/noticias/comunidade-quilombola-da-ilha-de-marambaia-tem-suas-terras -titulares, accessed on 25 September 2018.

9   https://en.wikipedia.org/wiki/Ubirajara_Alc%C3%A2ntara, accessed on 25 September 2018. A recent interview with the former player can be viewed at https://www.youtube.com/watch?v=JtEBTGIddYo. See also post: https:// tardesdepacaembu.wordpress.com/tag/ubirajara-da-silva- alcantara /, accessed on 25 September 2018.

10   https://pt.wikipedia.org/wiki/Dorival_Knipel accessed on 25 September 2018.

Updatism in a few characters

4.1. The evocation of history in Dilma Rousseff's impeachment

It is likely that the Radio Bandeirantes slogan, 'In 20 minutes everything can change', made sense in some moments of 2013 until the vote on Dilma Rousseff's impeachment and its unfolding in the successive and concentrated phases of the so-called 'Operation Lava Jato'. In this interregnum of time, in addition to references to fiction such as the *House of Cards* and the profiles of the series with Brazilian politics,[1] history has also been invoked several times. It has even been said that Dilma's speech in the Senate on the eve of her defeat was *for history*.[2] This perception seems to indicate that the speech was not intended to reverse the ongoing political process but merely to record a position. It is still interesting to think about the ambivalence of this judgement, since in Dilma Rousseff's speech the word 'history' appears eight times, almost all of them involving the idea of a historical process or even a 'historiography' or 'memory' capable of judging and redeeming.

> If some tear their past and negotiate the benefits of the present, let them answer before their conscience and before history for the acts they do. It is up to me to deplore for what they were and what they became. And resist. Always resist. Resisting to awaken dormant consciousness so that together we can set foot on the ground that is on the right side of history, even if the ground shakes and threatens to swallow us again. [. . .] Many people today ask me where my energy to keep going comes from. It comes from what I believe. I can look back and see everything we did. Look forward and see all that we still need and can do. [. . .] The most important thing is that I can look at myself and see the face of someone who, even marked by time, has

the strength to defend her ideas and rights. [...] Today Brazil, the world and history are watching us and are awaiting the outcome of this impeachment process. [...] The Constitution is invoked so that the world of appearances hypocritically covers the world of facts.[3]

While many watched the speech in 'real time', at least four documentaries were produced. In this regard, the Workers Party Senator Gleisi Hoffman, for example, said at the time that those who are planning a coup against Rouseff 'complain about film crews because they do not want the coup recorded in history. But yes, there will be a documentary with their smiley face.'[4] While in Dilma's speech history appears as a great force, one with an almost transcendent value, in the judgements about his speech the idea seems to prevail that it would be historical precisely because the dispute was already over and lost, its value being only testimonial. Somehow our question is: does this history still exist? Is it possible to separate the world of appearances from the world of facts, as Rousseff denounces in her speech?

Of course, a set of professionals – historians – create and write about a specifically historical past. But perhaps 'the historical past exists only in books and articles written by past professional researchers and directed largely to themselves – rather than to the general public' (White 2010, p. 125). For Hayden White, the paradox is that as historical studies become more scientific, they become less useful for any practical purpose, even for educating citizens for political life. According to Henrique Estrada Rodrigues (2016), it is actually about the following aporia:

If, on the one hand, the twentieth century witnesses the consolidation of the disciplinary form of history, 'our time' seems to indicate a horizon not only of retraction of the public sphere but also of some disbelief as to the relevance (or authority) of professionals of history. (Rodrigues 2016, p. 3)

In spite of the Eurocentrism of the term 'history' to designate the past experience, does some belief still survive that history (lived and thought) designates true and real processes? This modern idea of history ('history in itself and for itself'), as analysed by Koselleck (2006, 2014), was established in the West between the eighteenth and nineteenth centuries, and has as its basis a certain anthropocentrism, or rather a conception of humanity that separates man (and the word is that) from nature. Do these distinctions still hold?

4.2. Post-human, post-democracy?

Artificial intelligence rearranged its power grid into hexagonal patterns,
mimicking the human brain.

Caswell Barry 2018[5]

Some people take the risk of speaking about a post-human condition: 'the present technologies of death are posthuman due to the strong technological mediation through which they act' (Braidotti 2015, p. 20). In this direction, can the digital operator of a drone be considered a pilot? 'We all today are in a relationship with the world whose symbol would be the drone' (Castro 2014), that is, the consequences of actions are increasingly separated from the actions. The drone metaphor would also help explain the impeachment process: 'Dilma's dismissal is to democracy as are drones to war. Both reduce collateral damage caused by tanks firing on the streets. They have fragile legality and rely on manipulative evidence' (Conti 2016). We live in digital universes, eat genetically modified foods, use prosthetics and make use of reproductive technologies. All these current life dimensions blur the boundary of what is and is not human. Perhaps the common thread is the commodification of the human and nonhuman dimensions of current life.

Braidotti argues that Lyotard's 'modernist notion' of the inhuman has become a set of post-human and post-anthropocentric practices: 'the relationship between the human and the technological other, as the affections involved in it, such as the desire, cruelty and suffering, radically change with the current technologies of advanced capitalism' (2014, p. 132). She points to the confusion between the 'technological object' and the 'body' and the naturalization of the transitivity of the boundaries between genera, races and species already pointed out, according to her, by Lyotard: 'The *technological other* today – a mere ensemble of circuits and rings of feedback – moves in the social domain of the unfocused differences, if it does not touch even indeterminacy' (2014, p. 132).

From a more critical, militant and radical perspective, the Tiqqun[6] collective argues that we are moving from a sovereign paradigm of power (vertical, static, centralized) to cybernetic (horizontal, dynamic, distributed). The model for this new form of cyber governance would be Google or Facebook (Facebook today has 2.95 billion users, which is larger than China's population).[7] Cybernetics would be a new technology for government (Tiqqun 2013). From a more academic point of view, this governability has been called algorithmic (Rouvroy and Berns 2015). Canclini (2018, p. 93) also points out that self-exploitation with consensus has marked the current stage of capitalism and, more than in pre-digital times, has played a decisive role in reproducing exploitation.

Beyond Facebook, the power and control of information that Google has been accumulating is daunting. Until 2009, Google's main algorithm, PageRank, achieved the same results through link relevance. Since that time, the result is what the algorithm suggests is best for each one. The consequences of this change are well analysed in Pariser 2012, in particular as regards the action of trackers on data accumulation and private preferences. With regard to trackers, data on Brazil identified in 2010 the presence of '362 user data trackers [...] on only five Brazilian Internet sites (Terra, UOL, Yahoo, Globo.com, YouTube) and 295 trackers on the two most popular social networks in Brazil at the time (Orkut and Facebook)'. These tools are at the service of the online marketing, although more recently they have been organically integrated into political marketing. The tracking and archiving of our actions on the internet is made possible by the structure of this communication network, because 'every action leaves a potentially recoverable trail, constituting a vast, dynamic and polyphonic archive of our actions, choices, interests, habits, opinions, etc.' (Bruno 2016, p. 34). Still on these questions Canclini (2018) states:

> Many young people who use Snapchat to make messages that disappear seconds after being read, at the same time, accept cookies without warning [...]. No one wants to get out of the Internet altogether, but it requires a fine – collective – work learning to be a citizen: how to control what they want to know about us and what to do with what we don't know they do. (Canclini 2018, pp. 103 and 104)

Thus, more recent approaches seem less optimistic about the emancipating impacts of social networks. The optimism of US provider MCI's advertising in its famous add, first aired during the Superbowl break in 1997, remains one of the best examples of the optimistic outlook: 'There is no race, there are no genders, there is no age, there are no infirmities, there are only minds. Utopia? No, the Internet. MCI has the fastest internet connection.'

The possibility of anonymity that the mediation of the network promised that, soon after, with the rise of Web 2.0, would take the opposite direction, suggested the overcoming of the inconvenience of having a body. Applying Slavoj Zizek's concept of interpassivity to understand the nature of our Facebook interactions, Muhr and Pedersen come to the following conclusion:

> The inter-passive part of Facebook, therefore, is its ability to act as the video recorder that records the movies I want to see but never get a chance to watch. It postpones the encounter with my own passivity, my suffering and pleasure, while keeping the promise that when I finally do, it will be just as I had hoped. (Muhr and Pedersen 2010, p. 275)

From the standpoint of historicity, would we be going fast to nowhere (Rosa 2011; Martin 2016)? Would the resident of the digital panopticon be victim and actor at the same time? Would we live in a positive society of the 'I like'? For Byung-Chul Han, the crisis of the present age 'is not acceleration but rather the scattering and dissociation of temporality. Temporal dis-synchrony makes time buzz without direction and disintegrate into a mere succession of punctual, atomized presences' (Han 2013, p. 65). In this sense, the solution is not just to slow down or treat the current scene as more of the same in the oscillation between modernization and historicist compensation. From our point of view, the right question may perhaps be: in our updatist condition does everything get updated so that everything remains the same? Casanova seems to believe so, when he states that

> what is happening at every moment is [. . .] always too fluid to be named as event, even if it is only derivatively. Stagnation is our law, however much it may be experienced in an unceasingly dynamic environment. Everything changes here incessantly so that everything remains the same. As in Belchior's old song, which bears the beautiful title 'colorful old shirt': 'what was young, yesterday, today is old, and we all need to rejuvenate'. The problem is that this rejuvenation is of the unique and exclusive order of the colorful old shirt. (Casanova 2017, pp. 41–2)

According to Silveira (2017), also in the relationship with others the emergence of social networks involves promises and catastrophes, the exhibition of the self allows us to think about the expansion of empathy and understanding, a global public sphere fantasized in fiction by Tv Shows like *Sense8*, but 'it is also an instrument of humiliation' (Silveira 2017, p. 75). Still, the whole discussion of the rights-duties to exhibition involves the loss of control of what is shown and its scope, which leads us to forgetting and to analysing the risks in terms of an editable past or memory. What is the criterion of truth of this past or this memory? For Paula Sibilia (2018), the nineteenth-century registration mania nowadays has paradoxical proportions, since the ability to store is accompanied by the power to delete what was stored, claimed as a personal right:

> It is no coincidence that, just now, these dreams of an editable memory to the consumer's taste emerge, as if life itself were a story told in digital form, whose unpleasant episodes could be erased – or rather deleted – with the typical effectiveness of the computers and by one's free decision. [. . .] Now, both planes – life and audiovisual report – merge in this biography whose texture is informatics. Treated as digital archives, memories are no longer conceived as those ethereal and mysterious entities that, according to modern beliefs, nourished the interiority of each individual. (Sibilia 2018, pp. 219–20)

In this regard, it should be noted that the body of Jeremy Bentham (1748–1832) is still exposed in his chair at University College London. Andrew Keen (2012) is on the apocalyptic side of the effects of the so-called social revolution, which rather than emphasizing the liberating or transforming potential of the new media, highlights the risk involved in their irresistible expansion. It is curious that his essay appropriates the language of Twitter. The author sees Bentham's gesture of the continual exhibition of his body as an extreme symptom of the utopia of total transparency and total exhibition that would replace traditional forms of subjectivity with interiority.

For Keen, this new social is yet another way of isolating people so that they can function more fully as parts of a great productive gear. Social technologies would exploit modern man's passion for self-exposure by associating exposure with social value. In an increasingly individualistic and competitive world, social networks would make us new Benthams, trapped in our individual cell-showcase, but at the same time present in every exhibition space where we no longer know how to differentiate the individual camera from the camera-camera that imprisons. A possible consequence: the impoverishment of the experience that arises from a society that hinders privacy, interiority, with the different profiles of the men who are producing this great revolution of total (pseudo) digital presence and transparency. This profile, according to the author, would have as a mark of distinction the difficulty in assuming oneself as an adult, producing a juvenile *ethos* that would be one of the sources of the inability to face the experience of true solitude and privacy. Without disagreeing with Andrew Keen's pessimism, we can still believe that, within the humanities, we must stand up to the challenge of the complexity of experience. We can still make social media a tool, although it is undeniable that the movement expected by its producers and corporations is the opposite, namely that we become pieces of this new digital gear.

In this regard, Byung-Chul Han (2016) may help, when he points out some positivity in the phenomenon of *hikikomori*, which he calls 'a-social'. Young people, usually Japanese, who are isolated from society, but who maintain relationships through the computer. Would they be a new symbol of being together? According to the author, there are ongoing mutations opened by being-in-network. These transformations are analysed from a historical perspective by J. B. Thompson (2009, 2010) as capable of creating various mediated interactions, as they are not based on co-presence: 'electronic media enabled the transmission of information and symbolic content over long distances with little or even no delay. Hence, they create a kind of "despatialized simultaneity"' (2010, p. 22). One of the consequences of this process is what the author calls the 'changing frontier of public and private life' that can now lead, through the profusion of scandals, entire parts of political and social life to chaos (2010, p. 22).

In a horizon of questioning ideologies, perhaps we would have to learn to act and to do beyond parties, political programme and the logic of the assembly. To the German-Korean author, it is likely that Rousseau, given his inclination for solitude, if he lived today, was a *hikikomori*. The general will can rather be constituted mathematically without any communication, and at the same time be more just and representative. A democracy founded, in our view, by numerical transparency. Now, what we are talking about here is a real-time democracy. Is it really possible and desirable? The risks have been well worked out, too, by several episodes of the *Black Mirror* series.

Ivana Bentes (2016), in an analysis of the episode 'Nosedive', states: 'All social interactions are subject to a real-time assessment, which can be converted into more access and social advantages or into segregation.' The contamination of the political-social dispute by the logic of clickbait has caused real earthquakes in old structures of liberal democratic power. Whether in leaks such as those promoted by Edward Snowden or operations like the Car Wash operation, we can imagine the political, social and economic uses of this indiscriminate surveillance (Bentes 2016).[8] The 'monetization of youtubers', also addressed by Bentes, puts in question certain optimistic, participatory and democratic rhetoric of Web 2.0 and social networks, as the platform has become a space dominated by the major media corporations: 'YouTube allows the existence and creation of counter-hegemonic discourses in its own right. But it also exercises control over these by the possibility of censoring or eliminating them at any time' (Márques and Ardèvol 2018, p. 49).

Moreover, it must be reminded that in the asymmetric interaction between corporations and consumers we have, on the one hand, the transparency of the latter's data and, on the other, the opacity of the former's algorithms in the 'communicational age of capitalism' (Canclini 2018, p. 91). The paradox can be stated as follows: while in social networks gratification is immediate, 'representative democracy works differently: it does not generate immediate gratification, and, [. . .] it is not meant to do so. [. . .]. Hence the recent tendency to replace the party – unable to generate immediate gratification – by the movement'. According to the author, like networks, movements combine 'maximum horizontality' with leaders and vertical structures: 'Facebook is undoubtedly a horizontal network, but it is also, after all, Mark Zuckerberg's toy. [. . .] The same goes for Macron at En Marche!' (Barros 2018).[9]

Are we facing the impossibility of free relationship or even overcoming with the world of technique? For Duarte (2010), 'as more and more the real, nature, and man himself are technically produced, it will increasingly make sense to talk about virtual reality, virtual or artificial nature, and even man-made artificial virtualization' (p. 12). The author points out that Heideggerian philosophy does not advocate the end of technique, science or modernity. It is, in fact, a call to other uncertain and unpredictable possibilities of a freer relationship to these dimensions. Still, what is at stake in our time, therefore, is humanity itself, the birth and death of humans: what is the price of the elimination and/or postponement of death by technique? What being are we talking about more and more? From what openness, history, memory and forgetfulness? The almost integral planning, production and manipulation of birth and death is not only a fact of the fictional imagination of the Netflix series, it is also one of the realities and a present-future of our world. Is updatism the time of the virtualized real and, in this sense, the ambiguous promise of the end of the difference between the present (actual) and the virtual?

Despite using a different perspective from that adopted here, Castells (2011), in his analyses of what he calls network society, culture of real virtuality and timeless time, highlights the denial of death as one of the expressions of the current 'technological ambition and in accordance with our celebration of the ephemeral' (p. 547). This attempt to erase death from life or turn it into something meaningless is also the product of its repetition in the media, as the other's death: 'separating death from life and creating the technological system to make this belief last long enough, we build eternity during our existence' (2011). It would be an attempt to push mortality into an ever-postponed future: 'Over the past decade, the struggle for time has paved the way for the fundamental conflict of our society: a new culture of nature against the culture of the annihilation of time, which amounts to the cancellation of human adventure' (p. XXIX).

In this context, the very notions of hegemony and counter-hegemony are in question. In the current reconfiguration of power disputes, for Canclini (2018), ambivalent, hybrid combinations emerge in which various actors and forms of sociability intervene, 'in which power has no binary structure but a dispersed complexity. There are many ways of being together, of communicating and sharing or disputing the goods' (p. 95). Yet the unrealized utopia of the horizontal, free and democratizing dimension of income engenders a strong sense of powerlessness in citizens and consumers. The notion of resistance, from this perspective, also undergoes profound change. After all, 'who disturbs the machine the most: social movements or scattered hackers' (p. 98)? Furthermore, the future of many jobs will be a combination of computer processes with human tasks. Just think about Uber and Airbnb today. Apparently, this is a conducive system for working under updatist conditions. In addition, it should be said that most of the planet is already owned by nonhuman subjective entities (nations and companies). From Harari, in *Homo Deus*, Canclini (2018, p. 101) argues that *dataism*, that is, the religion of data, ultimately creates the belief in the invisible hand of the data stream.

But, on the other hand, citizenship actions arise that demand quality and truth of information. A fact, we would say, that explains, for example, the hiring of information-checking companies from Facebook for the 2018 elections in Brazil.[10] Algorithmic manipulation certainly arouses criticism, mobilization and feedback, but some fundamental questions remain open in the current process of robotization and economic concentration. 'Today's painful conflicts do not seem manageable with robotic governability programs' (Canclini 2018, p. 103).

Paradoxical as it may be, certain updatist dimensions of our contemporary life may also be the conditions of possibility for reflection and action on the various emergencies: gender, anti-racism, Eurocentrism, environmental issues, among others.[11] But they may also prevent us from seeing some of the contemporary global problems associated with the expansion of financial capitalism, such as global warming. The challenge is to rethink the humanities, since the theories of most of them are inadequate to the problems that surround us (cf. Domanska 2010). Would this imply thinking of knowledge in the humanities beyond anthropocentrism and emphasizing the collapse of the distinction between natural and human history? Thus, it would be necessary to rethink the nature/culture relationship and, for example, break the silence and emphasize that the current climate change is a human work (Chakrabarty 2013).

These questions certainly relate to what some authors call technical-scientific citizenship (see, in particular, Feenberg 2011, 2017). In this regard, Castelfranchi and Fernandes (2015) try to think about the current possibilities of resistance and confrontation: 'One of them is what we call insistence: a hacker policy, through which one does not see technology and domination as pervading imperatives that stand above outside us' (p. 191). They reinforce the ability of social actors to modify these structures through gestures of resistance and resignification through use, because these structures 'need to function sensitively to the real-time feedback from the behavior and desires of individuals who are consumers, voters, pressure groups, etc.' (Castelfranchi and Fernandes 2015).

4.3. *Black Mirror*, 'White Christmas': The collapse of historical time?

A smartphone is itself a much safer friend than a messy, unpredictable human being. Much less threatening to deal with and unwilling to change moods or halitosis.

(Harris 2014, p. 83)[12]

In one of the short stories from the episode 'White Christmas' of the British television drama *Black Mirror*, a patient wakes up after a medical procedure about which we have no information at first.[13] Her little mental dilemma is to anticipate that her eventual complaint about the slices of toast that were about to be served would produce an inescapable affliction. More toasted than to her personal taste, she had two options left, to eat without complaining or to return them to the attendant, who had just asked if everything was fine. Consumer of a high standard of service, the patient expects to be entitled to the small comforts of life, a personalized service. Having to ask and teach another human being about their preferences, which will surely look like incomprehensible banality, creates internal conflicts and anxieties that the current viewer can easily imagine. The scene resolves with the patient returning the toast and asking for more to be made. As expected, the attendant flashes a protocol smile, but leaves the room a little furiously at what seems to her a lot of fuss. On the other hand, the patient's perfect morning was definitely ruined by the distress of unpredictable and messy interaction.

In the next scene, we learn that the medical procedure in question was the upload of the whole of her memories to a computer, which then emulates the original personality. But the dystopian aspect, already anticipated in the harrowing description of a seemingly banal social situation, takes on unexpected shapes. The purpose of the procedure was to produce a perfect personal assistant, an exact copy of herself, able to anticipate all her desires, to know all her crazes, to feed all her vanities. This assistant, connected to every device in the house and all the gadgets that make up our new digital fauna, could enhance life by personalizing every aspect of her daily life. Everything could now be programmed, from the floor's temperature her feet will touch in the morning, the increasing brightness of the room upon waking, the toast's personal point, friends and the social interaction carefully mediated by a personal curator: perfect life as a comfort bubble.

The problem is that this set of digitally stored memories is itself a consciousness, a database-driven individuality and a processor, continually fed by inputs from its peripheral organs. Awakening in a completely abstract and homogeneous virtual environment, the copy does not know to be a copy, it believes to be the original consciousness of which it now exists apart. At this moment, a type of professional comes into play whose function is to explain to the new being its nature and what is expected of it in this new world into which it was thrown. The first reactions of the duplicate consciousness are disbelief, denial and revolt. How 'herself' could have done this, how to live forever in a virtual space for the sole purpose of serving someone, and after having lived a 'real' life, having known the pleasures and desires of a physical existence. But that is exactly why this consciousness becomes the ideal personal assistant, a quasi-person, or *a person abstracted from his/her human condition*.

In the episode, the dialogue between the 'programmer-overseer' (lived by actor Jon Hamm) and his victim (Oona Chaplim) is mediated by a kind of gadget with embedded peripherals like cameras and audio. The domestication tactics of the encapsulated consciousness, part of the dystopian setting, begin with the acceptance of its condition, which reaches its apex when consciousness sees its original body in an innocent afternoon nap. This recognition gives rise to great revolt and refusal to assume the role of eternal assistant reserved for her.

The programmer then moves to phase two, intimidation and torture. Since the virtual environment in which the emulated consciousness exists is completely controlled by its owners, it can have all its variables manipulated. Since emulated consciousness has no body, would traditional forms of torture make no sense, or appear ineffective without the risk of physical death? Thus, the manipulation of a completely empty and homogeneous virtual time is the ultimate source of manipulation, in fact the basis of all control. With a simple gesture on a console, the programmer is able to expand or contract the time experienced by duplicate consciousness. In the first section he subjects her to three weeks – twenty-one days – trapped in a non-environment, with literally nothing to do, not even the possibility of killing time sleeping. For the operator, only twenty-one seconds of chronological time passed. The consciousness returns from this forced experience in shock but still resists commands. It is then subjected to an even longer lapse of time, six months in the void, in the most terrible of the 'lonely cells'. When it returns, it is simply begging for something to do. At the same moment, the 'original consciousness' appears in the kitchen, where the battle had been fought, and asks:

Have you programmed yet? – All right, ready to start.

The episode fragment ends with another morning. With the concentrated dedication of her other self controlling all the variables of the environment, finally our protagonist can enjoy a perfect day: 16 December marks the agenda carefully displayed by her zealous assistant, who anticipates a day full of potentially rich human experiences, meeting friends for Christmas drinks, going to the theatre to watch *The Nutcracker*. The episode was produced as a Christmas special for TV, aired on 16 December 2014. More than a mere exercise in futurology, the drama is intended to be a reflection on our relationship to technology and the boundaries and contradictions of our humanity.

After all, can this copied and bodiless consciousness be understood as a human being? What happens to the concept of authenticity, the idea of proper being, when we are able to objectify ourselves? Does original consciousness remain original after its duplication?[14] In the end, does not all history seem to demonstrate an inability of this original self to relate to other human beings in an uncontrolled environment? At one point the programmer seems to suggest that the difference between the two versions would not be that one of them does not have a body, but that one of them is able to pay for the service, and has the legal prerogatives to do so. The true copy seems to be true only because it is able to pay for authentication. Enjoying the pleasures of having a body, of autonomy, becomes a privilege that many other people or entities would be deprived of.

The strange familiarity that the situation sometimes evokes, such as when the programmer presses the mute key during an opponent's verbal attack, stems from our growing familiarity with virtually mediated forms of communication. So when we are surprised to try to advance a video from a live stream and are extremely frustrated to realize that the future we want to advance to does not yet exist, it is not available in our present. The long sessions of the Brazilian Parliament and/or the Federal Supreme Court broadcast live in moments of great national commotion, which have recently become commonplace, have certainly been an inexhaustible source of this gesture, usually when watched through media such as the tablet, the computer or the mobile phone. Less tied to the logic of traditional open TV, replaced by streaming services like Netflix, Spotify, Google Play, iTunes and others, we automate control over what we're watching, making the real-time experience of the live a source of anxiety. It is a modality of the same sentiment that seems to be the central theme of the episode, how to live the real world, the historical world, when it so insistently seems to be out of our control, our ability to manipulate time, space and consciousness. But surely this is not a new desire or practice; it is worth remembering the social reactions to modern engineering of time, so well illustrated by Walter Benjamin in analysing vandalism against public clocks in the revolutionary waves of the nineteenth century.

On the other hand, living in a completely virtual world can mean a qualitative shift in this human tendency to formalize time. What the episode invites us to think about is the extent to which we are constantly being manipulated by our own desires. The complete appropriation of time that updatist experience promises, making it available to total manipulation, is the same gesture that makes time proper, historical time in the sense of a decided appropriation based on understanding and affective disposition. Scarce, and therefore valuable, time itself seems to be achieved only by the total alienation of the other, even when it seems to be a luxury to have someone automatically deciding for you. Experience seems like a privilege in a world where a certain aestheticism promises a total coincidence between the personal and the real. But this comfort bubble is just the other side of the same mirror such that all its black or all its white faces are equivalent. Alienated from itself in its two halves, consciences become slaves to each other: actress and viewer of herself in a reality as perfect as fiction. In the end, real life becomes a kind of highly addictive show for its copy, which keeps the routine of the original under control, spontaneously programmed as the script for a reality show.

Paradoxically, ego duplication is a response to our deep fear of loneliness and, at the same time, our dissatisfaction in our dealings with real people who resist our expectations. This duplicate consciousness is never alone, but it is never truly related to a reality it may miss. Updatism produces the feeling that everything that matters is or will be available and present. As Michael Harris has so well characterized, a whole generation of digital migrants witness and document, in the short span of a lifetime, the fastest and deepest technological transition we have ever heard of. To this generation, something seems to have been lost along this path, something that digital natives are unable to miss: 'What is this feeling of a mysterious loss that strikes us with every step we take on this path? I keep coming back to the loss of a fault, the end of absence' (Hafner 2016, p. 63). Or, 'In our race for the promises of Google and Facebook – for the promises of reducing ignorance and loneliness – we feel we are heading for a better life. We have forgotten the myriad accommodations we make along the way' (Hafner 2016, p. 71).

Loneliness arises in 'White Christmas' only as an extreme form of torture; in the neutral and homogeneous virtual space where the consciousness is imprisoned there is no time in its own right, so it seems unable to get lost in reflective reverie, there is no hint that it took this time for self-reflection.

This manipulated time, which is extremely fast in the outside world and extremely slow in the virtual world (but could be the other way around if the programmer so desired), does not allow the kind of daily suspension that Heidegger associates with the state of anxiety, which is also a confrontation with emptiness, but at the end of which we can decide and assume the world as our potentiality-of-being. Unable to be alone, because it has naturalized the world as something essentially external to itself, this pure consciousness sees in absence and loneliness (or solitude) only anxiety (see also, among others, Ferraris 2011; Turkle 2011; Sibilia 2016; Dunker 2017). In any case, the central story of the 'White Christmas' episode is exactly the drama of being placed in a restricted status housing, an euphemism by which prisons in the United States define the torture of the lonely cell.

4.4. Analog-digital cell: Isolation, exhibition and aging

An older generation than that of digital migrants seems to live today, at least in the central countries of capitalism, the effects of disengagement on non-digital community relations. In the article 'Researchers Confront an Epidemic of Loneliness', journalist Katie Hafner draws a grim picture. An increasing number of people over the age of sixty who end up living alone feel increasingly lonely. We know that being alone and feeling lonely are quite different things, it is possible for a 'lonely person to walk among the people' or to engage in deep relationships being alone. Often the pity that 'living alone' causes in our society ignores the potential sociability of being alone. In the digital world, we are less and less alone, but no less lonely. In both the United States and Great Britain, rates of loneliness, that is, among those people over sixty who claim to suffer from loneliness, range from 10 to 46 per cent, which has been motivating, especially in the British context, a growing concern with public and private initiatives aimed at addressing this reality. Hafner cites research conducted by University of California professor and geriatrician Carla Perissinotto with people over the age of sixty where 43 per cent report suffering from loneliness (Hafner 2016).

In a society where personal value goes through the ability to innovate or at least keep up to date with the continuous flow of innovations, the functions traditionally associated with aging seem to lose meaning. The atomization and personalization that new social technologies promise us depends on our ability to continually subscribe, as if our real self should correspond to a continually broadcasting virtual self. The desire to show off oneself seems to fit perfectly with the desire to see, in the unlimited curiosity about the most mundane aspects of everyday life, as proven by the success of services like Periscope, which allows any user to turn moments of their routine into video streams while watching live and whose motto is the phrase: 'see the world through someone else's eyes'. This desire for total empathy seems to mark the utopias and dystopias of updatist digital time.[15]

In 2016, one year after its launch, the service celebrated 200 million broadcastings, and 110 years of live video are watched daily (Team Periscope 2016). In the simple presentation on its website, the service reveals great ambitions: 'What if you could see through the eyes of a protester participant in Ukraine? Or watch the sunrise aboard a hot air balloon in Cappadocia? It may sound crazy, but we wanted to create something that was almost like teleportation.'

This new anxiety about fame has been well recorded by a recent British survey that compared the aspirations of today's children with those of a generation in the past. By 1990, the most cited careers were teaching, banking and medicine. Today, the three most desired professions for children in the UK are sportsman, pop singer and actor (This is not Advertising 2012).

Esse est percipi, to be is to perceive and to be perceived. The old maxim of the Irish philosopher George Berkeley (1685–1753) takes on unexpected shapes in our updatist condition. Constantly reproduced by various social media, like the work of art described by Walter Benjamin, our face value depends less and less on any kind of aura or cult of authenticity and more on our success in reproducing us in multiple copies whose original is no longer so easy to discern. The relationship between the original consciousness and its copy seems to be, in fact, the relationship between different modes of reproduction. Ultimately, it is the various services and applications that 'authenticate' and differentiate the original from the copy, as long as you continue to pay for them, in cash or in personal data that we constantly allow to be stored. Increasingly personal and thirsty for personalized services that feed on continual self-display, we feel unique, differentiated in the sense of being different and better, definitely set apart from something like the similar other. Always different but not diverse, social media feed on our loneliness and at the same time render us incapable of being alone in meditation.

The tendency to subjectivation is one of the most consensual traits of modernity, which has always had forms of subversion and criticism. The tourist/traveller visiting the Van Gogh Museum today, for example, can certainly experience how the painter deepened and subverted the self-representation that had and still has in Flemish portrait painting one of the great pillars of the affirmation of modern subjectivity. At the same time, how can we not think, from our perspective, of the contrast between the density and complexity of self-portraits inside the Van Gogh Museum or even the Flemish art gathered across the square at the Rijksmuseum and the frantically self-photographing crowd in diverse interactions with the huge sign on the lawn with the city's new brand 'I Amsterdam'.[16] In this regard, Byung-Chul Han (2013), in his radical critique states: 'the "human countenance" has long since disappeared from photography. The age of Facebook and Photoshop assures that the "human countenance" has become a mere *face* that equals only its exhibition value. [. . .] In the society of exhibition, every subject is also its own advertising object. Everything is measured by its exhibition value. The society of exhibition is a society of pornography. Everything has been turned outward, stripped, exposed, undressed, and put on show' (pp. 27 and 29).

Exploring the tensions and new complexities in the enactments of subjectivity and of time is a fundamental task, as the culture of self finds today ever more powerful media in which it feeds (itself).

In an article announcing a US government initiative to reduce and regulate the misuse of isolation in its prisons, Barack Obama responded to a lengthy national debate that denounced the fact that about 100,000 people were currently being held in lonely cells; some of them, around 25,000, for periods that could extend to years of confinement (Barack Obama 2016). Journalist Erica Goode produced a series of influential reports describing the state of prisoners and the trivialization of the practice, which was extended in the 1980s and 1990s, but whose foundations, as she recalls, go back to the Victorian imagination that believed that self-reflection brought about by loneliness would have educational effects on the prisoner (Tawile 2016). Some specialists who study the effects on prisoners of long periods of solitary confinement often relate their symptoms to the experience of social death.

Our current social state, with many friends and no friends, perhaps explains the success of the zombie figure (a quasi-alive or quasi-dead) in contemporary pop culture; never alone, we continue to suffer from loneliness and its effects, always divided between digital and non-digital lives, and it is not always easy to migrate from one environment to another.[17] The use of social networks can play a positive role in our ability to strengthen our social ties, but it has also served as a strategy that only compensates for the effects of loneliness, making us less able to take care of each other out of the bubbles of digital comfort. The growing sense of loneliness is compensated by the widening of our possibilities of connection, on which we are increasingly dependent. If, for Heidegger, the most defining human activity is caring for other human beings, feeling caring and caring is critical, networks promise to deliver us that feeling without the real-world commitments and problems. As with Periscope, seeing with others' eyes and then disconnecting generates a phenomenon of digital relationships called ghosting, already widely documented (Tawile 2016).[18] But, as Rodrigo Turin points out in his reading of one version of this text, one must understand better the emergence of new and intense forms of political solidarity and social ties that, for example, the new generations experience through occupations and collectives, where loneliness can be relativized and questioned through a positive transit between the virtual and the real.

Notes

1 See for example https://super.abril.com.br/cultura/5-vezes-em-que-house-of -cards-tirou-sarro-da-politica-brasileira/ accessed on 25 September 2018. Also see Pinto and Farias 2017.

2 Available on: http://agenciabrasil.ebc.com.br/politica/noticia/2016-08/confira -integra-do-discurso-de-dilma-em-julgamento-do-impeachment-no-senado, accessed on 25 September 2018.

3 Ibid.

4 Available on: https://www.brasil247.com/pt/247/poder/252049/Document %C3%A1rios-registram-o-golpe-para-a-hist%C3%B3ria.htm, accessed on 25 September 2018. One of these documentaries, 'O Processo de Maria Augusta Ramos', was the public's third favourite film at the Berlin International Film Festival (2018) in the Panorama section. The trailer can be seen at: https://www .youtube.com/watch?v=Z3rHUGdOXUs, accessed on 25 September 2018.

5 On https://www.tecmundo.com.br/software/130225-ia-deepmind-consega-find -saida-labirintos-virtuais.html. The study published in *Nature* can be read at

https://www.nature.com/articles/s41586-018-0102-6, accessed on 25 September 2018. About DeepMind, as well as AlphaGo's victory in Lee Sedol, see https://en.wikipedia.org/wiki/DeepMind, accessed on 25 September 2018 and the documentary AlphaGo. We highlight an excerpt from the Wikipedia article that states the purpose of the company Google acquired in 2014: 'The goal of "DeepMind Technologies" is "resolute intelligence", which they are trying to achieve by combining "the best learning machine techniques and neuroscience systems to build powerful learning algorithms with a generalized purpose". All this reminds us of a sceptical-melancholy comment by Baudrillard (1996) from the end of the last century: 'Today we do not think about the virtual, it is the virtual that thinks about us. And this imperceptible transparency that definitely separates us from the real is as incomprehensible to us as it can be to the fly the glass against which it collides without understanding what separates it from the exterior world. The fly doesn't even imagine what puts an end to its space. Similarly, we do not even imagine how much the virtual has already transformed, as in anticipation, all our representations of the world. We are unable to imagine it because it is in the nature of the virtual to put an end not only to reality but also to the imagination of the real, the political, the social – not just the reality of time but also the imagination of the past and the future (this is called, with a good deal of dark humor, "real time"). We are still far from understanding that the media's entering the scene avoids the evolution of history, that the rise to the stage of artificial intelligence prevents the advance of thought [. . .] In historical time, the event occurred and the evidence does exist. But we are no longer in historical time, we are in real time – and in real time there is no more proof whatever they might be [. . .] Real time is a kind of black hole where nothing penetrates without first losing its substance [. . .] This is exactly the defeat of thinking – of historical thinking and critical thinking. In fact, however, it is not its defeat: it is the victory of real time over the present, over the past and over all forms of logical articulation of reality [. . .] Now there is no thought of artifice in a world in which thought itself becomes artificial.'

6   Cf. http://tiqqunim.blogspot.com.br/. Cf., also, https://en.wikipedia.org/wiki/Tiqqun.

7   Cf., also, https://www.cartacapital.com.br/revista/941/qual-e-o-plano-do-facebook-para-dominar-o-mundo.

8   On Snowden and the issue of surveillance/control see Lyon 2015.

9   This passage is a critical dialogue of the author with Runciman (2018). In a recent interview Runciman foreshadows post-democracy as follows: 'Our world has changed a great deal over the past 30 years – changing the way we live on

almost every level except in democratic politics. Even the political upheavals of the past two years, from Brexit to Trump, are small changes compared to the impact Facebook is having on the human experience. At some point this change will reach democracy. The Cambridge Analytica scandal is just a glimpse of the new world to come – for better or for worse. [. . .] Democratic politics, which in big part of its history has been accused of being too volatile and timid, now often seems complicated and cumbersome. (See recent congressional attempt to question Zuckerberg: it was embarrassing.) [. . .] The great danger to democracy is the concentration of wealth and power with technical expertise – in technology, finance and universities. [. . .] America's post-democratic future is likely to imply the continuing fragmentation of its political identity. Politics will become both more local and more global, more individualistic and more connected, more populist and more technocratic. [. . .] Democracy will increasingly become empty idea'. Available at: https://www .bloomberg.com/view/articles/2018-05-22/democracy-s-death-narra-ted-by -david-runciman

10 The immediate attack by conservative groups such as the Free Brazil Movement (MBL) on fact checking, in the view of some analysts, already announced the 'virtual guerrilla' that should mark the Brazilian election. See http://piaui.folha .uol.com.br/lupa/2018/05/21/fgv-a-taques-eleicoes/, accessed on 25 September 2018.

11 See, among others, Silva 2014.

12 It should be noted that most smartphone programs and applications are produced, marketed and controlled by a select group of large corporations such as Google and Facebook.

13 This episode was written by Charlie Brooker, the series' creator.

14 Could we say that this consciousness, in societal or collective terms, is now called Google? In this regard, Paula Sibilia (2018, p. 229) states that 'the most widely used Internet search engine is not only a sort of all-knowing oracle, but also a legitimate – or at least legitimated – instance [. . .] – to manage the personal referrals of its millions of users around the globe'. Thus, the author goes on (p. 230): 'Truth has ceased to emanate from within, as we used to think until recently. Now it springs from someone else's gaze. This transit from a modern way of understanding memory to a contemporary and still coagulating form seems to be increasingly confirmed, even as regards to something fundamental: who one is, who one has been and who one could become.'

15 On the relationship between historical imagination and dystopia, see in particular Bentivoglio (2017).

16 https://thisisnotadvertising.wordpress.com/2012/11/05/i-amsterdam-the
-campaign-to-re-brand-amsterdam/, accessed on 25 September 2018.

17 Exhibitionism, voyeurism and the pursuit of fame find, according to Paula Sibilia
(2010, p. 55), 'fertile ground in a society atomized by an individualism with
narcissistic edges, which needs to see its beautiful image reflected in the eyes of
others to be. Loneliness in this picture, far from being exterminated, becomes a
difficult problem to solve: increasingly rare because it is increasingly intolerable,
it promotes substitutes such as the need for permanent connection and the
illusion of having "a million" of friends in the mirages of social networks'.

18 The practice of ghosting points to important transformations. In this regard,
Sibilia (2018, pp. 221 and 222) points out that: 'when operating according to
computer logic, if no one remembers that something happened – including
oneself – because this data was technically eliminated, then one can act as if it
had never happened. It is comparable to what happens when you use the scalpel
to shape your own physical appearance, for example, or when you practice
ghosting by blocking someone from all communication networks to end a
relationship without having to give boring explanations. [. . .] what we are loses
the solid consistency it used to bear, to become something much more flexible
and reprogrammable to one's taste. [. . .] almost nothing is stored forever, neither
in the impalpable interiority of the soul, nor in the privacy of the house'.

Loading – Provisional remarks

But what seems certain is that in both cases the delegitimation and preva-
lence of the performance criterion sound like the final hour of the Professor's
age.

(Lyotard 2009, p. 95)

It seems that surviving, resisting and opposing updatism implies producing
outdatings, rather than slowing down, as important as it is. In this regard,
Lyotard, in his 1979 essay, stated that the role of teaching and the university was
changing. Since the structures of postindustrial society rendered the search
for legitimacy obsolete, the university's justification for some kind of *bildung*
or wisdom formation would necessarily collapse, affecting in particular the
field of the humanities. It was no longer a matter of forming elites to guide
the nation, but of providing the system of players, that is, narrators capable of
updating the system's reports and routines (Lyotard 2009, p. 89). The answer
is one of adaptation, not of regret. It would be up to the university to offer
flowing knowledge, continuing education in pursuit of improved performance
within the system, and no longer the transmission of blocks of knowledge:
'and while the traditional teacher is assimilable to a memory, didactics can be
entrusted to machines articulating classic memories (libraries, etc.)' (Lyotard
2009, p. 92). What he considered as the possible destiny beyond the traditional
function of memory and processing would be a didactic whose importance
would lie on the 'ability actualize the relevant data for solving a problem "here
and now" and to organize that data into an efficient strategy' (Lyotard 2009, p.
93). What underpins Lyotard's optimism was that he could still imagine that
informational automatism would be incapable of routinizing the here and now
of updating.

Our bet in this book was that some fragments of modern and contemporary
temporalization can be approached around the updatism category. This bet was
based on the perception that one of the solutions to the crisis of the humanities

goes through a reflexive, critical and creative return to our possibility to theorize and develop new concepts.

At this point, we agree with Rosi Braidotti's (2015) analysis in her critique against the neo-empiricism in the humanities and the anti-intellectualism stimulated by neoliberalism: 'This is especially hard on the Humanities because it penalizes subtlety of analysis by paying undue allegiance to "common sense" – the tyranny of doxa – and to economic profit – the banality of self-interest. In this context, "theory" has lost status and is often dismissed as a form of fantasy or narcissistic self-indulgence' (p. 15).

Based on an intuition and interpretation of *Being and Time*'s chapter 'Temporality and Everydayness', we sought to present the hypothesis that certain aspects of the present time pointed out by some authors as symptoms of a historical mutation of experience may be derived from Heidegger's descriptions of temporality of disclosedness (*Erschlossenheit*), in particular of the inauthentic or improper dimension. As for Heidegger, these forms of experience are ontological; it was necessary to think about the meaning of their relative concealment in the descriptions of 'modern time' and their hypertrophy in the descriptions of the claimed novelty of our chronotope or regime of historicity.

Our attempt was also based on reflections that seek to relativize a homogeneous view of modern historicities. Throughout its existence, temporality identified as modern has been challenged by other, slower, faster historicities with other rhythms, other successions of events and other narratives (Jordheim 2014; Brito 2014). Thus, what we call updatism inherits part of its analytical vocabulary from various thinking traditions that have been sceptically and critically positioned to the modernization process. We have attempted to demonstrate this relationship in our Chateaubriand rereading, but it is evident that in a different way these same themes will reappear in more recent authors. The challenge is not to get carried away by a kind of fatalism, sometimes cynical, and thus obscure the emancipatory possibilities of these transformations.

Yet, after watching a series like *Billions*,[1] where the super-rich – the new Scrooge McDuck – update their fortunes in the game of financial and speculative capitalism in a blasé and amoral way, it is impossible not to agree that billionaires have given up the idea of a common world (Latour 2017). The difference seems minimal between one of the main characters, the speculator

'Bobby' Axelrod, and our real character, Joesley Batista. From this perspective one must consider that politics is by definition ecological, so the environment is not something external. Thinking about a world that can positively exploit, or even reverse, the same structuring forces that produce the present world needs to take these dimensions into account.

We believe that one of the problems with reflecting on presentism or the broad present is that those theories are not sufficiently aware of these different forms of the present, especially that any present will contain specific forms of past and future. To advance the characterization of deadlocks in the descriptions of our historicity, we believe we have argued and demonstrated that the concept and hypothesis of updatism help us to think of a form of the present that emphasizes improper temporalizations, which, even though always active at other historical moments, are becoming predominant not only in everyday life, as shown by the Heideggerian phenomenological description, but offer themselves as one of the hegemonic forms of temporalization in the digital age.

For now, we hope to have shown that our present need not be thought of merely as an extended present, or as a present without a future, but as a form of temporization grounded in a specific mode in which the present articulates past and future which we are provisionally calling updatism. Thus, we believe that we should think of our contemporary situation not as a negative statement, as having no future, a closed future or even a presentist future (and even a presentist past seen only from an extended present), but with a particular kind of future. Updatist past and future are not consumed solely on the basis of an extended present. This particular mode of articulation of temporal dimensions finds, as we have shown, in the temporality of falling prey an obvious kinship and helps us understand the paradox of a present that is both full of novelties and almost always empty of events. As much as these novelties present themselves, whether it comes from the past or the future, they are not capable of redoing conjunctural and structural links, because 'current time' (*atualidade*) makes itself present or updates itself (*se atualiza*) (almost) exclusively for the sake of the current time itself (*atualidade*). What this movement may bring back to the presentist argument is to clarify that it is not substantially a widening (or shortening) of the present, but even a widening of references to the past and future, but in an updatist mode. In this sense, the deepening of democracy (and citizenship), for example, can wait, because the important thing that the epigraph of the introduction highlights is the updating itself. Thus we can understand how the fashion or nostalgia of history and historical things or even of the past can be contemporary with the updatist experience of time. Or how a society that would have a closed future can be both addicted to news and eager for the latest Netflix series.

Note

1   Cf. https://en.wikipedia.org/wiki/Billions_(TV_series).

Afterword – Pandemic, fake news and updatism

In our experimental historiographical approach, we endeavoured to resist the constraints of a temporal paradigm that confines our thinking and feeling within the narrow boundaries of an updatist concept that denies any transformative potential to both the past and the future. By reintegrating the past and future into the present, and by restoring history as an active force that is not restricted to a lifeless past, we aim to reveal contingency and freedom as essential conditions of human action.

During the writing of the *Almanaque da Covid-19* (Pereira, Araujo, Marques 2020), we engaged in a series of public interventions to interpret the events of the day, acknowledging their fragmentary nature. These projections enabled us, as historians, to incorporate the future into our activism. At that point, we feared for the destruction of democracy fuelled by Bolsonarism, for example. Although at the time of writing this essay, those futures (yet?) remain unfulfilled and can only be experienced as past futures, they were concrete and possible at the time. Thus, an analysis of these histories finds its closest analogy in the image of a skein of temporalizations, where past, present and future can be combined in various ways, rather than a strict linear progression.

Despite our best efforts as historians to construct coherent narratives and explanations, the lived experience of history often resembles a cat playing with a ball of yarn, repeatedly returning the thread of events to its tangled, chaotic state. In this direction, our hypothesis is that consciously incorporating the present and the future into the writing of history can help us to go beyond the updatist agitation towards a critical posture of the reality of contemporary capitalism, without being limited to reactive and nostalgic strategies.

In the face of fear caused by Covid-19 and Bolsonarism, and as part of the Almanaque da Covid-19 project, we began public interventions through the Jornalistas Livres portal to explore the relationship between historicities and politics. Our initial aim was to reflect on the tragic and fatal encounter, for thousands of Brazilians, between the SARS-CoV-2 virus and Bolsonaro, and to avoid being consumed by constant updates. The *Almanaque*, which is a hybrid of chronology, diary, and chronicle, was also conceived as an archive of experiences that was created simultaneously with the pandemic event. In the absence of a consensual meaning, chronology and other writing genres with less interpretative demand allowed for the existence of an instantaneous book, which was written during the monstrous time of a monstrous event.

We believe that by analysing and describing historicities that are often overlooked due to updatism, we can activate and amplify more emancipatory historicities that exist within the whirlpool of history. The updatist strategy can only succeed if we accept its claim that it is the only way to exist in time. However, by recognizing and exploring alternative historicities, we can challenge this claim and open up new possibilities for how we understand and relate to the past, present and future.

We want to bring back to reflection (repetition can be a historical form of updating) some themes that emerged from the confrontation between updatism and the pandemic. We emphasize that unlike the organization of *Almanaque da Covid-19*, in which chronology served to give some sense that would resist the pressure for dispersion, here we intend to condense some themes without the pretence of representing these phenomena as copies of real processes. They are, therefore, fragments of anachronistic experience and thought, as we do not expect their meaning to arise from their own position in linear time. Somehow, putting these reflections back on a timeline would disfigure the fact that, for the authors, they already inhabit a plane of simultaneities that could only very violently be broken.

On the updatist politics

The Covid-19 pandemic serves as a reminder that we need to reevaluate our relationship with animals, the environment and the natural world. This reevaluation is more important and pressing than ever before. Among so many reasons is the fact that pandemics originating from zoonoses are directly linked to the articulation between human life and other forms of life as they are also ecological crises and, therefore, related to anthropocene times, with the times of history, capitalism and the current climate crisis.

In terms of life and practical wisdom, the experience of this existential catastrophe, that is, the Covid-19 pandemic, and its daily evidence, lead us to review the certainties of what was said and done the day before. This means that what seems right to be done now may be out of date tomorrow: 'both people's conceptions and assessments of experts made today can be outdated tomorrow' (Jordheim et al.).

It is in this context that, very quickly, journalists, scientists and intellectuals began to publish texts about the virus, in particular, based on European reality. We observe that many of them are still elaborated under certain colonial logics of the geopolitics of consumption and intellectual/scientific production, which often means taking a priori the 'centre' as the place of elaboration of theories and the 'periphery' as the place of data collection and application of results.

From our perspective, it is interesting to consider whether the Covid-19 outbreak suspends, transforms, problematizes and potentially radicalizes the different dimensions of updatism. One of the consequences of the pandemic has been the deepening of the connection between modernist historicity and contemporary capitalism in its constant mutations. Capitalism adapts and reproduces this catastrophic event through the multiplication and intensification of digital control over society, as well as the ruin of certain aspects of life and political institutions in the modern sense, as several analyses of contemporary capital and labour have shown, as noted in the reflections of scholars such as Shoshana Zuboff, Thomas Piketty, Paulo Arantes and Ricardo Antunes. Therefore, the updatist frenzy can be understood as both an anti-political and a new (and alarming) form of politics emerging from capitalist societies in the digital age.

In regard to the emergence of the Covid-19 pandemic, it is our belief that there was a significant misinterpretation of the virus in the West between January and February 2020. Many believed that it would be similar to the SARS-CoV-1 outbreak, but as Covid-19 continued to spread and its danger became more apparent, most countries began to follow the World Health Organization's instructions. However, in Brazil, the president was in conflict with his own health ministers, denying the severity of the pandemic and promoting reckless behaviour, which could lead to an increase in the number of infections.

In countries like Brazil and the United States, the tragedy of the pandemic was aggravated by its temporal coincidence with national governments openly denying its existence. In the Brazilian case, Bolsonaro was elected openly claiming to defend a supposed historical legacy of the civil-military dictatorship installed in Brazil in 1964, which lasted until 1985. Negationism as a form of politics became also a mode of government. Celebrating the military dictatorship, denying or justifying its crimes, became part of the same discourse that systematically denied the existence and severity of the Covid-19 pandemic. In the Brazilian case, the denialist epidemic was anchored, among other forms, in the conviction of impunity symbolized and authorized in the Brazilian Amnesty Law issued in 1979 by the military in preparation for redemocratization. An update of this story took place in 2020, through the authorization, by the Brazilian Supreme Court, of the celebration of the 1964 coup, posted on the Ministry of Defence's website.

However, Bolsonaro never admitted to being anti-science, but, on the contrary, claimed to be defending a 'true' science. After all, bolsonarist denialism grew from 2014 in reaction to the work of a National Truth Commission established by the Dilma Rousseff government to investigate the crimes committed by Brazilian state agents during the Military Regime. This initiative brought to light the memory of a community that denied the Brazilian authoritarian past and its violence (Pereira, 'Nova Direita?', pp. 863–902; Rocha 2021).

Pandemic, acceleration and fake news

Apparently, our experience of this existential catastrophe is not limited to a supposed acceleration of historical time, whether synchronous or not. As Ramalho argues, moments of crisis are also moments of accelerated change. Crises can be related to acceleration but they are not limited or reduced to it. Thus, the theme ends up greatly limiting the analysis of the crisis experience. Furthermore, various strata of the acceleration of modern time are also largely asynchronous. Thus crediting a good part of the current transformations to a supposed change in the regime of acceleration of modernity can make us incur several mistakes, in particular, the one of 'inflating' the theme and the perception of the phenomenon, that is, of reducing the crisis to just one of its layers and dimensions.

Our argument is confirmed by the fact that for certain people, social networks end up imposing some kind of updatist work rhythm. Thus, the person wakes up thinking they are going to do something they had planned, but the flow of the networks takes them in other directions, causing dispersion and agitation rather than acceleration. So they can't decide, they can just surf or not on the wave that takes them, as well as on the current epidemic wave, in another direction or even nowhere. Not only the virus epidemic affects us but also the *infodemia*, which already existed before and seems to have been intensified by the emergence of the new coronavirus.

It is also possible to notice a tendency to believe that the most current information is always more true, which often means that a news item is not verified for its veracity before being widely shared. What is experienced is agitation or even illness. Maybe that is why the idea of acceleration – synchronized or not – seems to be insufficient to think about this event. In other words, we are within a viral/epidemiological temporality and, consequently, of epidemic diseases and their multiple times of contagion, mortality and emergencies, which gains specificity in view, for example, of the various forms of contemporary mobility, changes of current capitalism and the technological/digital revolution.

In addition to the large number of deaths and people infected, the experience of this existential catastrophe also affects a greater number of people due to the agitation and transformation that the experience of isolation implies, as it creates changes in ordinary life (the so-called 'normality'), in our habits, daily lives and experiences. In this regard, we highlight that, between mid-March and April 2020, more than one-third of humanity was subjected to some type of isolation.

If on the one hand certain aspects of modernist historicity seem to resemble a radicalization of modern trends, fitting into the perspective of hyper-acceleration, on the other hand the questioning, deregulation and loss of autonomy of subsystems such as religion, politics and the media reveal a side of updatism that seems to dissolve fundamental structures of modernity, leaving in its place a vacuum continuously activated by agitation more than just different accelerations.

The virus updatist dimension

On 9 February 2020, the Chinese government had just delivered the second hospital for Covid-19 patients, built in record time. However, the hope that

Covid-19 might be less lethal than its predecessor began to unravel as the death toll in China reached 811, surpassing the global total for the 2002–2003 SARS epidemic. Despite past experience with similar outbreaks, it was clear that the contingency and novelty of this event posed unprecedented challenges.

Throughout the month of February, the virus was being downplayed by many. Even when Italy announced the quarantine of 50,000 individuals on the 21st of the month, some saw it as unnecessary alarmism. Meanwhile, in Brazil, others pointed out that we should be more concerned about the return of measles, which is more contagious than Covid-19 (Rossi and Buono website), or dengue, which posed a greater threat. At that time, 87 per cent of newly infected cases were still concentrated in China. However, within just two weeks, the situation changed dramatically, prompting the World Health Organization to declare the pandemic on 11 March. Past experience did not prepare us for the contingency and novelty of the event, and the gravity of the situation soon became clear.

On 26 February 2020, we posed a question: 'Is the coronavirus an "updatist" virus?' This enquiry stemmed from a report featuring epidemiologist Wanderson Oliveira, who was responsible for leading Brazil's efforts to combat the virus on behalf of the Ministry of Health. Oliveira warned that we were in the midst of an 'infodemic', an epidemic of misinformation, much of it false (BBC NEWS website). The Brazilian epidemiologist cautioned that the information was constantly evolving, as new evidence emerged before the system could even adapt to the previous data. From the perspective of both news reporting and the pandemic's own dynamics, it appears that the updatist logic was only intensifying. Oliveira himself admitted that the data was slipping through their fingers, as they were trying to contain a rapidly evolving epidemic in real time (Tribuna website).

Time, epidemiology and denial

The initial expectation of most world health authorities that Covid-19 would be a repetition of SARS-Cov-1 may have been due in part to a limited, perhaps even historicist, conception of historical time that is often employed in epidemiological analyses. This criticism of the restricted view of historical time in epidemiology has been raised by Brazilian epidemiologist Gil Sevalho since the end of the last century. Sevalho argues that such a perspective operates a cut in time based on statistical analysis, which amputates the historicity and temporal multiplicity of social and historical aspects involved in the complexity of collective human illness. By considering these dimensions, epidemiological thinking could be opened up to a better or even alternative understanding of emerging infections and the relationship between humans and nature. This means taking into account processes of non-linear determination, as well as dynamic systems that are constantly changing.

It is important to acknowledge the value of the hegemonic epidemiological reason, despite the challenges and limitations it faces. The current crisis has highlighted both its strengths and weaknesses. For instance, in Brazil, the experience with previous epidemics such as H1N1, at least until mid-March 2020, had prepared the country better for Covid-19 (Agência Brasil website). However, it is important to note that this does not mean that the hegemonic epidemiological reason is infallible. For example, a virologist responsible for discovering the Zika virus at that time downplayed the impact of Covid-19 in Brazil and wrongly claimed that the virus could not survive in the heat (Correio 24 Horas website). This highlights the importance of being open to new information and continuously updating our understanding of emerging infections, as well as the complex social and historical factors that shape them.

The accumulation of experience also came with the time and pace of diffusion of the epidemiological tsunami. This is a statement that serves Brazilians, but also many other people. This sensation was very well summarized in the headline of a Portuguese newspaper, shown at the end of March: 'Covid-19 in Portugal. On the way to the unknown and trying to delay the pace' (Nunes website). A headline, a synthesis, an observation: that we lived in a moment when delaying the pace may be more prudent than the quick arrival to an uncertain future.

Bolsonaro updated his discourse for any of the possible final scenarios regarding the pandemic: if social isolation works, he will say that Covid-19 was really just a 'little flu'; if the pandemic has devastating effects for Brazil, they could falsely blame the Chinese for the virus, say that the quarantine did not work and blame the defenders of social isolation – such as mayors and governors – for the economic downturn. Or, they can benefit from the impact of the corona voucher. Bolsonaro is also up to date as he reinforces the ideas that elected him and strives to appear in the demonstrations in his favour, maintaining a constant campaigning atmosphere, even though he has held the position of president for over a year. (In November 2020, Bolsonaro denied calling Covid-19 a flu, even though he did it twice publicly in March.)

Thus, throughout March and April, several countries, including Brazil (Schuquel 340–8), in part inspired by the Chinese and South Korean models, set up and expanded their strategies to fight the pandemic based on people's surveillance practices, for example, in relation to mobility, control of body temperature, gestures, heartbeat and also phone calls and virtual access, among other actions (on the Chinese 'model' see, for example, Rossi website). However, this is not about the efficiency of pandemic control based on the dichotomy between Dictatorships and Democracies (Fukuyama).

At the end of March, Imperial College London estimated that containment measures adopted in eleven European countries had managed to prevent 59,000 deaths (Flaxman et al. website). At that point, it was already possible to glimpse the local dimensions of this global tragedy, even because the virus itself was already reaching powerful people.

Wars of cultural updates and the crisis of statues

Like Donald Trump and Boris Johnson, some people fear that the toppling of statues could mean an erasure of history. But the truth is that many statues were already 'extinguished' in everyday life and only returned to being part of the collective memory at the time of their overthrow. Furthermore, these acts are photographed, filmed and widely shared on the internet; thus, it can be said that, although the statue is no longer present in the city, it can remain present in the memory through these media, and the debate and the moment of its overthrow can be used as opportunities for historical education and reflection on social values. The accusation of erasure, made by those who consider the removal of statues an act of vandalism, disregards that history, lived and thought, is made up of revisions/updatings.

Discerning revisionism from negationism seems important to us: we assume that negationism simulates a legitimate project of revision and, in this sense, it is clearly related to the type of lie we associate with disinformation, in particular with fake news. Revisionism that distorts and conceals is a negationist strategy as it operates not only false facts, but also distorted interpretations, arguments and values to defend a certain political position (Pereira, 'Nova Direita', pp. 863–902 and Pereira, Bianchi and Abreu 'Historicidades Democráticas', pp. 279–315; Rocha 2021).

However, we cannot consider that all revisionism is a negationist strategy or even that the only strategy of negationism is to dress up as revisionism. The reinterpretations of history are part of its production process, being necessary and often welcome. Historiography, here understood as the writing of professional history, generally moves from revisions of inherited knowledge, whether motivated by internal movements to the discipline or by transformations in the historical process itself.

In Brazil, the current denialist wave, which brought to light the nostalgia related to the dictatorship and the loss of authority of historians, professors and scientists in general, collaborated in the election of Bolsonaro in 2018. In general, negationist politicians have as strategy the fight against false enemies, the dissemination of conspiracy theories and regressive fantasies in which the country needs to go back to being a fictitious 'before' in the name of the possibility of an undemocratic future project.

As these fantasies do not solve the real problems these politicians must continue to fantasize incessantly. Very different from this historical, scientific and ethical negationism is revision, that is, honest historical revisionism, which seeks to bring out the complexity of the past, showing that no historical period is homogeneous or free from criticism. History is always reformulated as well as other sciences that develop from the discussion and discovery of new sources, problems and theories.

Updatist loopholes

In her 1972 essay *Lying in Politics*, Hannah Arendt analyses the so-called Pentagon Papers, a collection of reports produced by US agencies detailing the backstage of political decisions for the Vietnam War. The secret reports were leaked in a 1971 *New York Times* report, causing widespread and negative repercussions. For Arendt, the reports showed how the organized and systematic manipulation of lies could corrupt democracy based on practices of 'defactualizing' reality, replacing judgement by calculating probabilities and seeking psychological manipulation instead of concrete results in public services policies.

Arendt denounced that one of the goals of the Nixon administration was to discredit the press before the 1972 elections. In the philosopher's description, the scandal of the use of lies as systematic public policy was only possible due to the self-deception produced by the bubble effect in the conjunction between public agencies and mutually reinforcing *think tanks* who tried to convince society of the validity of their own fantasies. These fantasies met a well-informed public opinion by a credible press with its operative limit. Finally – and still of interest to our investigation – Arendt writes that while reading the reports she had the impression that computers and not 'decision makers' had been released in Southeast Asia (168). This automated character represented the belief in a conception of history in which contingency could be fully eliminated.

Perhaps what we have called updatism has an obvious relationship with this emerging ethos identified by Arendt and its epidemic spread made possible by the weakening precisely of institutions such as the press and specialists. Perhaps, in 2020 the ambiguities and contradictions of this process gained unprecedented visibility, a fact that also contributed to the possibility of the emergence of counter-updatist gaps that were dispersed or latent.

Thus, in view of the reflections of the aforementioned anachronistic fragments and, based on our investigations, throughout 2020, we came to the conclusion that what we call updatism was reinforced, not without ambivalence, by certain aspects of the experience of the pandemic in Brazil, such as: (a) isolation/loneliness, driven by quarantine and home working; (b) greater dependence on digital and surveillance capitalism structures; (c) anxiety for updates, fuelled by infodemic and political crisis; (d) dissemination of cultural wars and their logic based on (mis)information; (e) normalization of distraction, agitation, confusion and noise as strategies of (anti)political debate. This does not mean that, in parallel, individuals and institutions are not reacting to this deepening of the updatist environment, as it is visible in the alliance with the old policy that Bolsonarism ended up embracing after being threatened on several fronts, as well as in the partial brakes on the destructive and authoritarian Bolsonarism project by the legislature, judiciary and the press in its traditional and digital forms.

If we are right, we still have the challenge of dealing with one more question: How to reflect on the counter-updatist gaps in the current situation? We believe that we historians need to be aware of other emerging, unconventional and undisciplined historicities. There are, therefore, counter-updatist gaps in the situation described in a fragmented way above, namely: (a) demand for action in the crisis and its kairological potential (Ramalho, 'Historical time', 1–16); (b) the disclosure of environments and structures of surveillance capitalism with its entry into the political agenda via, for example, regulatory projects; (c) the insertion, even if unwillingly, of 'obsolete left-wing' sectors in the digital universe, even though it is too early to think about their legacy, as there are ambivalences in this immersion; (d) emergence of new forms of political organization (collective) that can present a counter-updatist potential and take us beyond the historicist traditional approach.

Thus, one of our main tasks is to reactivate stories in the homogeneous fabric of updatist historicity. Not only to produce more stories because somehow there is even an excess of updatist stories and pseudo-stories, updatism is not lacking in history as it is still a human phenomenon. What we need is to open space and reactivate other layers and forms of non-updatist historicity that can help us live better.

As incoherent as it may seem, the parallel universe of Trumpism manages to make sense of this agitation in an environment in which other systems seem to exist only to translate it. Perhaps the word 'simulation' is the key, as even the *NewsMax* cannot fail to look like a real news network, although it has none of what in modernity guaranteed journalism its place among the institutions of democracy. Ultimately, this notion of simulation helps us to understand how the history produced by the new right, even when it does not use denial, only simulates the procedures of an academic historiography. Without this simulation it would lose effectiveness, which does not mean that we can confuse this production with what produces the historical discipline – as it was constituted – as one of the structures of modern national states.

A counter-updatist path claims the present as an unavoidable part of the historian's work (rescuing, for example, the *Annales* legacy of a history from the present), but with a renewed emphasis on understanding the past and the future as time's gifts or assets which are not only available to the present, but which form a part of our existential environment. Thus, it is not just treating the present as a space for a specialized historiography – although this is also relevant – but as a transversal dimension in any historicization effort. Firmly resist the trend which was already present in certain derivations of historicism, that history is the science of the past, an idea that is anchored in everyday experience that naturalizes the identification of history with a dead past.

Perhaps we should return to the idea of process, as long as it is not applied to a totalizing and global understanding of reality. Human history is also formed by regional, sectorial processes, which can offer an important understanding of non-updatist duration, of highlighting the effects of past and future in the present, without reintroducing the image of history's train and its astonished avenging angel as an involuntary passenger.

Bibliography

Aarão Reis, Daniel. 'Notas para a compreensão do bolsonarismo'. *Estudos Ibero-Americanos* 46, no. 1 (2020): 1–11.

Abreu, Marcelo. 'Estátuas em transe: iconoclasmo e assimetrias na produção da história'. *Exporvisões* 29 (June 2020), https://exporvisoes374227711.wpcomstaging .com/2020/06/29/estatuas-em-transe-iconoclasmo-e-assimetrias-na-producao-da -historia/.

Agamben, Giorgio. *O que é o contemporâneo e outros ensaios*. Chapecó: Argos, 2009.

AGÊNCIA BRASIL. 'Fiocruz: Brasil está mais preparado contra Covid-19 que contra H1N1'. *UOL VIVA BEM* 1 (março, 2020). www.uol.com.br/vivabem/noticias/ redacao/2020/03/01/fiocruz-brasil-esta-mais-preparado-contra-covid-19-que -contra-h1n1.htm (Acesso em: 30 nov. 2020).

Alencar, José de. In *Lynch Conservadorismo caleidoscópico: Edmund Burke e o pensamento político do Brasil*, edited by E. C. Christian, 337. São Paulo: Lua Nova, 2017.

Ankersmit, Frank R. *Meaning, Truth and Reference in Historical Representation*. New York: Cornell University Press, 2012.

Araujo, Valdei L. de. 'A formação do regime de autonomia avaliativo no Sistema Nacional de Pós-graduação e o futuro das relações entre historiografia, ensino e experiência da história'. *Anos 90*, Porto Alegre 23 (2016): 83–109.

Araujo, Valdei L. de. 'Die Beobachtung beobachten: Über die Entdeckung der historischen Stimmung und dem Auftauchen des historistischen Chronotops um 1820'. In *Zweiter Ordnung im Atualismo 1.0: como a ideia de atualização mudou o século XXI | 232 | Historischen Kontext: Niklas Luhmann in Amerika*, 1st edn, edited by Perla Chinchilla Pawling, Aldo Mazzuchelli, and Hans Ulrich Gumbrecht, 99–114. Munique: Wilhelm Fink Verlag, 2013a.

Araujo, Valdei L. de. 'História da historiografia como analítica da historicidade'. *História da Historiografia* 12 (2013b): 34–44.

Araujo, Valdei L. de. 'História dos Conceitos: problemas e desafios para uma releitura da modernidade Ibérica'. *Almanack Braziliense* 7 (2008): 47–55.

Araujo, Valdei L. de. 'O Direito à História: O(a) Historiador(a) Como Curador(a) de Uma Experiência Histórica Socialmente Distribuída'. In *Conversas sobre o*

Brasil: ensaios de crítica histórica, edited by Géssica Guimarães, Leonardo Bruno, and Rodrigo Perez, 191–216. Rio de Janeiro: Autografia, 2017.

Araujo, Valdei L. de. 'Para além da auto-consciência moderna: a historiografia de Hans Ulrich Gumbrecht'. *Varia História* 22 (2006): 314–28.

Araujo, Valdei L, Pereira, Mateus Henrique de F. and Marques, Mayra. 'Almanaque da COVID-19: 150 dias para não esquecer ou a história do encontro entre um presidente fake e um virus real.1. ed. Vitória: Milfontes, (2020).

Arendt, Hannah. *A Condição Humana*. Rio de Janeiro: Ed. Forense Universitária, 2000.

Arendt, Hannah. *Crisis of the Republic*. Boston: Houghton Mifflin Harcourt, 1972.

Avelar, Alexandre S., Daniel A. B. Faria, and Mateus H. F. Pereira. 'Introdução História Intelectual do Brasil República: desafios contemporâneos'. In *Contribuições à história intelectual do Brasil Republicano*, edited by Alexandres Avelar, Daniel A. B. Faria, and Mateus Pereira, 12–26. Ouro Preto: EDUFOP, 2012.

Barros, Celso Rocha de. *O Brasil e a recessão democrática*. Piaui, 2018. http://piaui .folha.uol.com.br/materia/o-brasil-erecessaodemocratica (Acesso em 25 set. 2023).

Baudrillard, Jean. *A alucinação coletiva do virtual*. Disponível em: http://www1.folha .uol.com.br/fsp/1996/1/28/mais!/3.html (Acesso em: 25 set. 2018).

Baudrillard, Jean. 'Após a orgia'. In *A Transparência do Mal. Ensaio sobre os fenômenos extremos. Tradução de Estela dos Santos Abreu*, 9–19. Campinas: Papirus, 1996.

BBC NEWS. 'Epidemia ou 'infodemia'? A guerra de versões sobre o coronavírus na Europa'. *BBC NEWS*, 27 fevereiro 2020. www.bbc.com/portuguese/internacional -51666948 (Acesso em: 20 nov. 2020).

Benites, Afonso. Jairo Nicolau: 'Bolsonaro é uma liderança inequívoca. É um Lula da direita'. *EL PAÍS*, 27 setembro, 2020.

Bentes, Ivana. *Os odiadores da nação. Cult*. 2016. Disponível em: https://revistacult .uol.com.br/home/os-odiadores-danacao/ (Acesso em: 25 set. 2018).

Bentivoglio, Julio. 'C. A história conceitual de Reinhart Koselleck'. *Revista de História (UFES)* 24 (2010): 126–44.

Bentivoglio, Julio. *História e Distopia: a imaginação histórica no alvorecer do século XXI*. Serra: Editora Milfontes, 2017.

Berry, David M. *Copy, Rip, Burn: The Politics of Copyleft and Open Source*. London: Pluto Press, 2008.

Berry, David M.. *Critical Theory and the Digital*. New York: Bloomsbury, 2014.

Berry, David M.. *The Philosophy of Software: Code and Mediation in the Digital Age*. London: Palgrave Macmillan UK, 2011.

Bevernage, Berber. *History, Memory, and State-Sponsored Violence: Time and Justice*. New York: Routledge, 2012.

Blocker, Déborah and Elie Haddad. 'Le présent comme inquiétude: temporalités, écritures du temps et actions historiographiques'. *Revue d'Histoire Moderne et Contemporaine*, Belin Publishing 53 (2006): 160–9.

Boym, Svetlana. 'Mal-estar na nostalgia'. *História Da Historiografia*, Ouro Preto 23 (2017): 153–65.

Braidotti, Rosi. *Lo Posthumano*. Barcelona: Editorial Gedisa, 2015.

BRASIL 247 (on-line). *Documentários registram o golpe para a história*. 2016. Disponível em: goo.gl/ZQ6GxQ (Acesso em: 09 set. 2016).

Brito, Thiago *Vieira de. O Despertar da Presença: A Tensão Epistemológica Na Filosofia Da História de Gumbrecht*. Dissertação (Mestrado em História). Programa de Pós-Graduação em História Social das Relações Políticas. Universidade Federal de Espírito Santo, Vitória, 2014.

Bruno, Fernanda. 'Rastrear, classificar, performar'. *Ciência e Cultura*, Campinas 68, no. 1 (2016): 34–8.

Cameron, Robert M. *Update: A Utility Program for the An/gyk-3(v) Modular Data Processing System*. Washington, DC: Defense Technical Information Center/Naval Research Lab, 1967.

Canclini, Nestor G. 'Cómo investigar la era comunicacional del capitalismo'. *Desacatos*, México, CIESAS 56 (2018): 90–105.

Cantanhêde, Eliane. 'Conciliar o inconciliável'. *Estadão*, São Paulo, 14 ago. 2016. Disponível em: https://goo.gl/7aY55s (Acesso em: 09 set. 2016).

Cardoso, Ana C. M. 'Direito e dever à desconexão: disputas em torno dos tempos de trabalho e de não trabalho'. *Revista da Universidade Federal de Minas Gerais*, Belo Horizonte 23 (2016): 62–87.

Casanova, Marco Antônio S. *A falta que Marx nos faz*. Rio de Janeiro: Via Verita, 2017.

Casanova, Marco Antônio S.. *Mundo e historicidade: Leituras fenomenológicas de Ser e Tempo*. Rio de Janeiro: Via Verita Ltda, 2017.

Castelfranchi, Yurij and Victor Fernandes. 'Teoria crítica da tecnologia e cidadania tecnocientífica: resistência, insistência e hacking. Aurora: Revista de Filosofia (PUCPR. Impresso)'. *Curitiba* 27, no. 40 (2015): 167–96.

Castells, Manuel. *A sociedade em rede*. São Paulo: Paz e Terra, 2011.

Castells, Manuel. 'The impact of the Internet on Society: a global perspective'. In *Ch@nge: 19 Key Essays on How Internet is Changing Our Lives*, edited by Yochai Benkler et al., 127–47. Madrid: BBVA, 2013.

Castro, Eduardo Viveiro de and Déborah Danowski. 'Diálogos sobre o fim do mundo'. *El país*, 29 set. 2014. Entrevista concedida a Eliane Brum. Disponível em: https://goo.gl/F7b6X6 (Acesso em: 09 set. 2016).

Certeau, Michel. *A invenção do cotidiano: Artes de fazer*. Petrópolis: Vozes, 2008.

Cezar, Temístocles. 'Entre Antigos e Modernos: A Escrita Da História Em Chateaubriand. Ensaio Sobre Historiografia e Relatos de Viagem'. *Almanack* 11 (2010): 26–33.

Cezar, Temístocles. *Ser historiador no século XIX: o caso Varnhagen*. Belo Horizonte: Autêntica, 2018.

Chakrabarty, Dipesh. 'Antropocene Time. History and Theory'. *Middletown* 57 (2018): 5–32.

Chakrabarty, Dipesh. 'O clima da história: quatro teses'. *Sopro, Cultura e Barbárie* 91 (2013): 2–22.

Chateaubriand, François-René de. *Mémoires D'outre-Tombe. Tome Onzième*. Paris: Eugène et Victor Penaud Frères, 1850.

Chateaubriand, François-René de. *Memoires D'outre-Tombe. Tome Premier*. Paris: Librarie Garnier Frères, 1848.

Choay, Françoise. *A Alegoria Do Patrimônio*. São Paulo: Unesp, 2006.

Chun, Wendy Hui Kyong. *Programed Visions: Software and Memory*. Cambridge, MA: MIT Press, 2011.

Chun, Wendy Hui Kyong. *Updating to Remains the Same: Habitual New Media*. Cambridge, MA: The MIT Press, 2016.

Clarke, Arthur C. *2001: uma odisseia no espaço*. São Paulo: Aleph, 2013.

Clarke, Arthur C.. *Profiles of the Future: An Inquiry into the Limits of the Possible*. New York: Harper & Row, 1962.

Clarke, Arthur C.. *The Collected Stories of Arthur C. Clarke*. Londres: Victor Gollancz Ltd, 2000.

Clarke, Arthur C. and Ray Bradbury, ed. *Marte e a Mente Do Homemd: a conquista de Marte e o futuro do homem*. Rio de Janeiro: Editora Artenova SA, 1974.

Compton, William David and Charles Benson. *Living and Working in Space: A History of Skylab*. Washington, DC: NASA, 1983.

Conti, Mário Sérgio. 'Impeachment está para a democracia como drones estão para guerra'. *Folha de São Paulo*, s.d. Disponível em: https://goo.gl/3YKksZ (Acesso: 9 set. 2016).

CORREIO 24 HORAS. 'Farmacêutico alerta 'Estamos focando no coronavírus e esquecendo da dengue'. *Pfarma*, 8, março, 2020. pfarma.com.br/noticia-setor-fa rmaceutico/saude/5220-alerta-coronavirus-dengue.html (Acesso em: 30 nov. 2020).

Debord, Guy. *A Sociedade Do Espectáculo*. Lisboa: Editora Antígona, 2005.

Delacroix, Christian. 'Généalogie d'une notion'. In *Historicités*, edited by Christian Delacroix, François Dosse, and Patrick Garcia, 29–45. Paris: Éditions La Découverte, 2009.

Domanska, Ewa. 'Beyond Anthropocentrism in Historical Studies'. *Historien* 10 (2010): 118–30.

Duarte, André. *Vidas em risco: crítica do presente em Heidegger, Arendt e Foucault.* Rio de Janeiro: Forense Universitária, 2010.

Dunker, Christian Ingo Lenz. *Reinvenção da Intimidade: políticas do sofrimento cotidiano.* São Paulo: UBU, 2017.

Faria, Daniel. 'Anamorfose de um dia: o tempo da história e o dia 11 de dezembro de 1972'. *História da Historiografia*, Ouro Preto 8 (2015): 11–29.

Faria, Felipe. 'O Atualismo entre uniformitaristas e catastrofistas'. *Revista Brasileira de História da Ciência* 7, no. 1 (2014): 101–9.

Feenberg, Andrew. *Agency and citizenship in a technological society. Lecture presented to the Course on Digital Citizenship.* Copenhagen: IT University of Copenhagen, 2011.

Feenberg, Andrew. *Technosystem: The Social Life of Reason.* Cambridge, MA: Harvard University Press, 2017.

Felipe, Eduardo Ferraz. 'Renovar votos com o futuro: nostalgia e escrita da história'. *História da Historiografia*, Ouro Preto 10 (2017): 117–34.

Ferraris, Maurizio. *Dove sei? Ontologia del telefonino.* Milano: Bompiani, 2011.

Foucault, Michel. *As Palavras e as Coisas. Uma arqueologia das ciências humanas.* São Paulo: Martins Fontes, 2000.

Fuchs, Christian and Fisher Eran. *Reconsidering Value and Labour in the Digital Age.* Londres: Palgrave Macmillan, 2012.

Gentili, Giovanni. *Teoria generale dello spirito come atto puro.* Firenzi: Casa Editrice Le Lettere, 1987.

Goode, Erica. 'Prisons Rethink Isolation, Saving Money, Lives and Sanity'. *New York Times*, Nova York, 2012. Disponível em: https://goo.gl/Q7Nwes (Acesso em: 25 set. 2018).

Goode, Erica. 'Solitary Confinement: Reporter's Notebook'. *New York Times*, Nova York, 2015. Disponível em: https://goo.gl/eKT9Wn (Acesso em: 25 set. 2018).

Gumbrecht, Hans Ulrich. 'Cascatas de Modernidade'. In *Modernização Dos Sentidos.* edited by Hans Ulrich Gumbrecht, 9–32. São Paulo: Editora 34, 1998.

Gumbrecht, Hans Ulrich. *Graciosidade e Estagnação: Ensaios Escolhidos.* Rio de Janeiro: Contraponto: Ed. PUC-Rio, 2012.

Gumbrecht, Hans Ulrich. *Nosso amplo presente: o tempo e a cultura contemporânea.* São Paulo: Edusp, 2015.

Gumbrecht, Hans Ulrich. *Our Broad Present: Time and Contemporary Culture.* New York: Columbia University Press, 2014.

Gumbrecht, Hans Ulrich. 'Presence Achieved in Language (with Special Attention given to the Presence of the Past)'. *History and Theory*, Middletown 45 (2006): 317–27.

Gumbrecht, Hans Ulrich. *Produção de presença. O que o sentido não consegue transmitir.* Rio de Janeiro: Contraponto e PUC-Rio, 2010.

Gumbrecht, Hans Ulrich. *The Powers of Philology Dynamics of Textual Scholarship*. Chicago: University of Illinois Press, 2003.

Hafner, Katie. 'Researchers Confront an Epidemic of Loneliness'. *The New York Times*, New York, 5 set. 2016. Disponível em: https://nyti.ms/2VQGreQ (Acesso em: 25 set. 2018).

Han, Byung-Chul. *No Enxame: Reflexões Sobre o Digital. Lisboa: Relógio D'água, 2016. La sociedad de la transparencia*. Barcelona: Herder, 2013.

Han, Byung-Chul. *The Transparency Society*. Stanford: Stanford University Press, 2015.

Hannoum, Abdelmajid. 'What is an order of time?'. *History and Theory*, Middletown 47 (2008): 458–71.

Harris, Michael. *The End of Absence: Reclaiming What We've Lost in a World of Constant Connection*. New York: Penguin, 2014.

Hartog, François. 'Entrevista: François Hartog'. *Revista Brasileira de História*, São Paulo 35, no. 70 (2015): 281–91.

Hartog, François. *Croire en l'histoire*. Paris: Flammarion, 2013.

Hartog, François. 'Entrevista com François Hartog: história, historiografia e tempo presente'. *História da Historiografia*, Ouro Preto 10 (2012a): 351–71.

Hartog, François. 'Présentisme plein ou par défaut?'. In *Régimes d'historicité: Présentisme et expériences du temps*, edited by Hartog, François. Paris: Seuil, 2012b: I–V.

Hartog, François. *Régimes d'historicité: Présentisme et expériences du temps*. Paris: Seuil, 2003.

Hassan, Sara E. 'Los Gadgets. Acheronta Revista de Psicoanálisis y Cultura'. *Psicomundo*, Buenos Aires 7 (Julio, 1998): 12–21.

Heidegger, Martin. *Being and Time*. New York: State University of New York Press, 2010.

Heidegger, Martin. *Sein Und Zeit*. Tübingen: Max Niemeyer Verlag, 2006.

Heidegger, Martin. *Ser e Tempo*. Petrópolis: Vozes, 1993.

Heidegger, Martin. *Ser y tiempo*. Madrid: Trotta, 2003.

Jordheim, Helge. 'Introduction: Multiple Times and the Work of Synchronization'. *History and Theory*, Middletown 53, no. 4 (2014): 498–518.

Júnior, Guilherme S. G. 'Paisagem, Graça e Sentimento Do Belo: Winckelmann, Chateaubriand E Girodet'. *ARS*, São Paulo 12, no. 23 (2014): 80–103.

Kavaratzis, M. and G. J. Ashworth. 'I Amsterdam – The Campaign to Re-Brand Amsterdam'. *This Is Not Advertising* (Blog), 2012. Disponível em: https://goo.gl/oU3A69 (Acesso em: 25 nov. 2018).

Keen, Andrew. *Digital Vertigo: How Today's Online Social Revolution Is Dividing, Diminishing, and Disorienting Us*, Kindle edn. London: Constable, 2012.

Kleinberg, Ethan. 'Haunting History: Deconstruction and the Spirit of Revision'. *History and Theory*, Middletown 46, no. 4 (2007): 113–43.

Kleinberg, Ethan and R. Ghosh, eds. *Presence: Philosophy, History, and Cultural Theory for the Twenty-First Century*. Ithaca: Cornell University Press, 2013.

Koselleck, Reinhart. *Crítica e Crise: uma contribuição à patogênese do mundo burguês*. Rio de Janeiro: EDUERJ; Contraponto, 1999.

Koselleck, Reinhart. *Estratos do tempo: estudos sobre história*. Rio de Janeiro: Contraponto/Pontifícia Universidade Católica do Rio de Janeiro, 2014.

Koselleck, Reinhart. *Futuro Passado: Contribuição à semântica dos tempos históricos*. Rio de Janeiro: Contraponto/Ed. PUC-Rio, 2006.

Latouche, Serge. *Usa e Getta: Le Follie Dell'obsolescenza Programmata*. Torino: Bollati Boringhieri, 2015.

Latour, Bruno. *Les super-riches ont renoncé à l'idée d'un monde commun*. Paris: Bibliob, 2017. Disponível em: https://bibliobs. nouvelobs.com/idees/20170316 .OBS6702/bruno-latour-lessuper-riches-ont-renonce-a-l-idee-d-un-monde-co mmun. html (Acesso em: 25 set. 2018).

Lessalt, B. and F. Hartog. 'Régimes d'historicité. Présentisme et expérience du temps'. *L'Orientation scolaire et professionnelle* 33, no. 3 (15 set. 2004): 479–83.

Lewis-Kraus, Gideon. 'The Great A. I. Awakening How Google Used Artificial Intelligence to Transform Google Translate, One of Its More Popular Services — and How Machine Learning Is Poised to Reinvent Computing Itself'. *The New York Times Magazine*, 14 dez. 2016. Disponível em: https://goo. gl/dJaA3R (Acesso em: 25 set. 2018).

Lynch, Christian E. C. 'O Império é que era a República: a monarquia republicana de Joaquim Nabuco'. *Lua Nova: Revista de Atualismo 1.0: como a ideia de atualização mudou o século XXI | 244 | Cultura e Política*, São Paulo 1 (2012): 277–311.

Lyon, David. *Surveillance After Snowden*. Cambridge: Polity Press, 2015.

Lyotard, Jean-François. *A Condição Pós-Moderna*. Rio de Janeiro: José Olympio, 2009.

Lythgoe, Esteban. 'Disposición Afectiva Y Temporalidad En Martin Heidegger entre 1927 y 1930'. *Aurora*, Curitiba 26 (2014): 759–75.

Lübbe, Hermann 'Esquecimento e historicização da memória'. *Estudos Históricos* 29 (2016): 285–300.

Malerba, Jurandir. 'Acadêmicos na berlinda ou como cada um escreve a história: uma reflexão sobre o embate entre historiadores acadêmicos e não acadêmicos no Brasil à luz dos debates sobre a Public History'. *História da Historiografia* Ouro Preto, 15 (2014): 27–50.

Malerba, Jurandir. 'Os Historiadores e Seus Públicos: Desafios Ao Conhecimento Histórico Na Era Digital'. *Revista Brasileira de História*. São Paulo 37, no. 74 (2017): 135–54.

Malpas, Simon. *Jean-François Lyotard*. London: Routledge, 2003.

Marques, Danilo Araujo. *No Fio Da Navalha: Historicidade, Pós-Modernidade e Fim Da História*. Belo Horizonte: Ed. UFMG, 2017.

Márquez, Israel and Elirenda Ardèvol. 'Hegemonía y contrahegemonía en el fenómeno youtuber'. *Desacatos: Revista de Antropologia Social*, México 56 (2018): 34–49.

Martín, Estefanía Dávila. 'Rápido a ninguna parte. Consideraciones en torno a la aceleración del tiempo social'. *Acta sociológica*, México 69 (2016): 51–75.

Menzel, Christopher. *Actualism. Stanford Encyclopedia of Philosophy: Center for the Study of Language and Information*. Stanford University, 2014. Disponível em: http://plato.stanford. edu/entries/actualism (Acesso em 25 set. 2018).

Milner, Max and Claude Pichois. *Histoire de La Littérature Française de Chateaubriand à Baudelaire*. Paris: Flammarion, 1996.

Muhr, Sara L. and Michael Pedersen. 'Faking It on Facebook'. In *Facebook and Philosophy: What's on Your Mind?*, edited by Homero Gil de Zúñiga and Sebastian Valenzuela, 265–75. Chicago: Open Court, 2010.

Nicodemo, Thiago Lima. 'Requiém da interpretação do Brasil: o Ensaísmo em tempos de golpe'. In *Conversas sobre o Brasil: ensaios de crítica histórica*, vol. 1, edited by Gessica Guimarães, Leonardo Bruno, and Rodrigo Perez, 67–82. Rio de Janeiro: Autografia, 2017.

Nicolazzi, Fernando. 'A história entre tempos: François Hartog e a conjuntura historiográfica contemporânea'. *História: Questões & Debates*, Curitiba 53 (2010): 229–57.

Nicolazzi, Fernando. 'A História E Seus Passados: Regimes Historiográficos E Escrita Da História'. In *Escrever História: Historiadores e Historiografia Brasileira Nos Séculos XIX E XX*, edited by Julio Bentivoglio and Bruno César Nascimento, 7–36. Vitória: Milfontes, 2017.

Obama, Barack. 'Why We Must Rethink Solitary Confinement'. *The Washington Post*, 2016. Disponível em: goo.gl/WBL5ga (Acesso em: 25 set. 2018).

Oliveira, Bernardo. 'A personagem de ficção e o mundo digital'. *Viso: Cadernos de Estética Aplicada* 17 (2015a): 204–20.

Oliveira, Bernardo. 'As narrativas seriadas e a experiência contemporânea'. *O Que nos Faz Pensar (PUCRJ)*, Rio de Janeiro 36 (2015b): 299–314.

Palti, Elías José. *"Giro lingüístico" e historia intelectual: Stanley Fish, Dominick Lacapra, Paul Rabinow y Richard Rorty*. Buenos Aires: Universidad Nacional de Quilmes, 1998.

Pariser, Eli. *O filtro invisível: o que a internet está escondendo de você*. Rio de Janeiro: Zahar, 2012.

Pereira, Mateus and Araujo, V. Vozes sobre Bolsonaro: esquerda e direita em tempo atualista ISBN 9786586207002. In: Klein, Bruna; Araujo, Valdei; Pereira, Mateus.

(Org.). Do fake ao fato: Des(atualizando) Bolsonaro. 1ed. Vitória: Milfontes (2020): 115–40.

Pereira, Mateus H. F. 'Nova Direita? Guerras de Memória Em Tempos de Comissão Da Verdade (2012-2014)'. *Varia Historia*, Belo Horizonte 31, no. 57 (2015): 853–902.

Pereira, Mateus H. F. and Valdei L. de Araujo. 'Actualismo y presente amplio: breve análisis de las temporalidades contemporáneas'. *Desacatos, Revista de Antropología Social* 55 (2017): 12–27.

Pereira, Mateus H. F. and Sérgio Mata. 'Introdução'. In *Tempo Presente & Usos do Passado*, edited by Mateus H. F. Pereira and Sérgio Mata, 9–30. Rio de Janeiro: FGV, 2013.

Pereira, Mateus H. F., Pedro A. C. Santos, and Thiago Nicodemo. 'Brazilian Historical Writing in a Global Perspective: A Study on the Emergence of the Concept of Historiography'. *History and Theor*, Middletown 53 (2015): 84–104.

Phillips, Mark Salber. *Society and Sentiment: Genres of Historical Writing in Great Britain, 1740-1820*. Princeton: Princeton University Press, 2000.

Pimenta, João Paulo. 'História do presentismo, história presentista? A propósito de Regimes de historicidade, de François Hartog'. *Revista de História*, São Paulo 172 (2015): 399–404.

Pinto, Luiz C. and Luisa Farias. *A arte imita a vida: Análise do seriado de TV "House of Cards" sob o olhar da comunicação e sua relação com a política. XIX Congresso de Ciências da Comunicação na Região Nordeste*. Anais . . . Fortaleza: Intercom, 2017.

Plant, Sadie. *The most radical gesture*. New York: Routledge, 1992.

Rangel, Marcelo M. de. 'Sobre a utilidade e desvantagem da ciência histórica, segundo Nietzsche e Gumbrecht'. *Dimensões*, Vitória 24 (2010): 208–41.

Rangel, Marcelo M. de and Thamara O. Rodrigues 'História e Modernidade em Hans Ulrich Gumbrecht'. *Redescrições*, Rio de janeiro 4, no. 1 (2012): 63–71.

Ribeiro, Gustavo, org. 'Dossiê: La hegemonía del capitalismo electrónico-informático'. *Desacatos: Revista de Antropología Social,* México, 56 (2018): 16–33.

Ricoeur, Paul. 'A marca do passado'. *História da Historiografía*, Ouro Preto 10 (2012): 329–49.

Ricoeur, Paul. *A memória, a história e o esquecimento*. Campinas: Editora da Unicamp, 2007.

Ricoeur, Paul. *Tempo e narrativa. t. III*. Campinas: Papirus, 1997.

Rigney, Ann. 'When the Monograph is No Longer the Medium: Historical Narrative in the Online Age'. *History and Theory*, Middletown 49, no. 4 (2010): 100–17.

Rocha. *João Cezar de Castro. Guerra cultural e retórica do ódio: crônicas de um Brasil pós-político. 1.* ed. Goiânia: Editora e Livraria Caminhos, 2021.

Rodrigues, H. E. O conceito de formação na historiografia brasileira. In: MEDEIROS, Bruno Franco; SOUzA, Francisco Gouvea de. BELCHIOR, Luna Halabi; RANGEL, Marcelo de Mello; PEREIRA, Mateus. (Org.). Teoria e historiografia: debates contemporâneos. 1ed. Jundiaí: Paco Editorial, (2016): 253–71.

Rosa, Hartmut. 'Aceleración social: consecuencias éticas y políticas de una sociedad de alta velocidad desincronizada'. *Persona y Sociedad*, Chile, Universidad Alberto Hurtado XXV, no. 1 (2011): 9–49.

Rosa, Hartmut. *Social Acceleration: a new theory of modernity*. New York: Columbia University Press, 2013.

Rousseff, Dilma. *Discurso no Senado*. 2016. Disponível em: https://goo.gl/Gydg1a (Acesso em: 09 set. 2016).

Rouvroy, Antoinette and Thomas Berns. 'Governamentalidade algorítmica e perspectivas de emancipação: o díspar como condição de individuação pela relação?'. *Revista Eco Pós*, Rio de Janeiro 18, no. 2 (2015): 35–56.

Rumyantzeva, Mary. *Compensation-Theory in the Context of Classical and Contemporary Conception of Modernization Process: Dualistic Model of Modernity, Proposed by Odo Marquard and Hermann Lübbe*. Higher School of Economics Research Paper, 2018.

Runciman, David. *How Democracy Ends*. New York: Basic Books, 2018.

Santos, Pedro A. C,, Thiago L. Nicodemo, and Mateus H. F. Pereira. 'Historiografias periféricas em perspectiva global ou transnacional: eurocentrismo em questão'. *Estudos Históricos*, Rio de Janeiro 30, no. 60 (2017): 161–86.

Schmidt, Benito B. and Mara C. Rodrigues. 'M. O Professor Universitário de História É Um Professor? Reflexões Sobre a Docência de Teoria e Metodologia Da História E Historiografia No Ensino Superior'. *História Unisinos* 21 (2017): 169–78.

Sevalho, Gil. 'Tempos históricos, tempos físicos, tempos epidemiológicos'. *Cadernos de Saúde Pública (ENSP. Impresso)* 12, no. 3 (1997): 7–20.

Sibilia, Paula. 'Celebridade para todos: um antídoto contra a solidão?'. *Ciência e Cultura* 62 (2010): 52–5.

Sibilia, Paula. *O show do eu: a intimidade como espetáculo*, 2nd edn. Rio de Janeiro: Contraponto, 2016.

Sibilia, Paula. 'Você é o que Google diz que você é: A vida editável, entre controle e espetáculo'. *Intexto*, Porto Alegre 42 (2018): 214–31.

Silva, Regina Helena A. da, org. *Ruas e redes: dinâmicas dos protestos BR*. Belo Horizonte: Autêntica, 2014.

Silveira, Pedro Telles. *Registrar. Arquivar. Imaginar. Possibilidades teóricas em busca de uma crítica da história digital na cultura histórica contemporânea. Qualificação (Doutorado em História)*. Porto Alegre: Universidade Federal do Rio Grande do Sul, 2017.

Sim, Stuart. *Lyotard and the Inhuman: Postmodern Encounters*. London: Icon Books, 2001.

Tawile, Mia. 'Ghosting, a New Social Phenomenon Caused by Digital'. *Marketing & Innovation* (blog), 2016. Disponível em: https://goo.gl/2WjRgg (Acesso em: 25 set. 2018).

TEAM PERISCOPE. 'Year One'. *Periscope Blog*, 2016. Disponível em: https:// goo.gl/ TdD5BG (Acesso em: 25 set. 2018).

Thompson, Johan B. *A mídia e a modernidade*. Petrópolis: Vozes, 2009.

Thompson, Johan B. 'Fronteiras cambiantes da vida pública e privada'. *MATRIZes*, São Paulo 4, no. 1 (2010): 11–36.

TIQQUN. *La hipótesis cibernética*. 2013. Disponível em: http://tiqqunim.blogspot .com.br/2013/01/la-hipotesis-cibernetica.html (Acesso em: 25 set. 2018).

TRIBUNA ONLINE. 'Escorre pelas mão'. *Tribuna Online*, 26 fevereiro 2020. Disponível em: tribunaonline.com.br/escorre-pelas-maos (Acesso em: 20 nov. 2020).

Trüper, Henning. 'Löwith, Löwith's Heidegger, and the Unity of History'. *History and Theory*, Meddletown 53, no. 1 (2014): 45–68.

Turin, Rodrigo. 'A polifonia do tempo: ficção, trauma e aceleração no Brasil contemporâneo'. *ArtCultura*, Uberlândia 19, no. 35 (2017): 65.

Turkle, Sherry. *Alone together: why we expect more from technology and less from each other*. New York: Basic Books, 2011.

Ungureanu, Camil. 'Aestheticization of politics and ambivalence of self sacrifice in Charlie Brooker's The National Anthem'. *Journal of European Studies*, VALERO, Aurelia (2015): 114–33.

Werner, Michael and Bénédicte Zimmermann. 'Penser l'histoire croisée: entre empirie et réflexivité'. *Annales*, Paris: EHESS 58, no. 1 (2003): 7–36.

White, Hayden. *Ficción histórica, historia ficcional y realidad histórica*. Buenos Aires: Prometeo Libros, 2010.

Zawdzki, Paul. 'Les equivoques du présentisme'. *Esprit*, Paris 345 (2008): 114–34.

Zermeño-Padilla, Guillermo. 'História, Experiência e Modernidade na América Ibérica, 1750-1850'. *Almanack Braziliense*, São Paulo 7 (2008): 5–46.

Zermeño-Padilla, Guillermo. 'La historia en un tiempo "presentista"'. *Desacatos*, México 55 (2017): 8–11.

Index